THE DEAD MILKMEN

ALSO AVAILABLE

Brainiac by Justin Vellucci

De La Soul by Dave Heaton

AFI by Andi Coulter

Fountains of Wayne by Fiona McQuarrie

Laughing Hyenas by Steve Miller

The Apples in Stereo by Josh Bloom

Sammy by Jeff Gomez

THE DEAD MILKMEN

Tyler Sonnichsen

J-Card Press

ISBN: 979-8-9917394-6-7 (print)
ISBN: 979-8-9917394-7-4 (ebook)

Library of Congress Control Number: 2026937714

J-Card Press
460 Center Street #6578
Moraga, California 94570

Cover photo by Chris Coccia
Designed by Malory Keaton

www.jcardpress.com

For Dave Blood

Photo courtesy of Kurt Schulthise

We shall not defeat Amerika [sic] by organizing a political party. We shall do it by building a new nation—a nation as rugged as the marijuana leaf.
—Abbie Hoffman, Youth International Party

Let this be the start of our revolution . . .
—The Dead Milkmen, "Prisoner's Cinema"

CONTENTS

PROLOGUE: DEAN'S DREAM

July 1983. Manayunk, Northwest Philadelphia.

Dave Reckner and Dean Sabatino roll down Baker Street as sirens blare in the distance. *Was that a gunshot?* They pull up to the house at 4445. It's a shithole in a rough neighborhood, but this is what $400 a month will get a bunch of Temple students. He may be out of office (thank God), but it's still Rizzo's Philly. It's *all* bad neighborhoods. They'd heard an interesting fellow named Frank—most believed his parents were siblings—wanders the block "listening" to a broken radio. *OK, that* was *a gunshot.*

They get out and start unloading Dean's drums. It's been a few months since his band, Narthex, called it quits. Well, his bandmate Mike "fired" himself, and he was the only other member, so . . . Maybe one day, Dean will have his own home studio, but for now, it's cool somebody wants to jam. Maybe if things work out, he can play the East Side Club again, maybe put a real record out, maybe even tour? Suddenly, not much is keeping Dean in Upper Bucks County. Sure, his parents are cool with some noise, his graphics job at the thermostat company is fine, and his "wearable art" show in Pennridge got some press, but no more being a big fish in a small pond. No idea if this will change things, but for now, he has a date with the Dead Milkmen.

Joe, one of Reckner's friends from Temple, had apparently made a bunch of silly tapes with his friends out in Coatesville. For the past year, Joe had been writing songs with David, a dude six years their senior who used to live in this shitty house—at least, he did when they came to that party last Christmas. Joe and David spent that winter working on this new tape with another guy from Coatesville, and they'd given Dean one of the ten copies. *What is up with that cover art? Is Elvis supposed to be on fire?* The songs are a mess. One song about fish sounded like the Sex Pistols banging on a bucket. *Was that the only percussion they had?* Some songs make fun of Republicans and the NRA—Dean can get behind that. Songs about junkies, death, and abortions, though . . . *Who wrote this stuff?*

They load Dean's drums into 4445 Baker Street and banter while he sets up. Almost immediately, it's unclear who's auditioning for whom. Joe and David are shocked that this guy, with actual drum cases and everything, would consider joining their band after hearing that tape. They have trouble keeping up with a seasoned drummer, but Dean doesn't mind. Sure, he'll practice with these two again. They're making him laugh. This is kind of fun.

Reckner looks on and tries not to cringe. It's pretty much the worst thing he's ever heard.

December 1983. A chilly Saturday afternoon in Ridley Park.

David's parents are out of town, and to annoy their asshole neighbors, they've encouraged their son to bring his fledgling band to practice in their Clymer Lane duplex. The Dead Milkmen have a lot working against them—no convenient rehearsal space, Joe and Rodney are both still in college (and Rodney's still under twenty-one)—but things are gaining traction. Rodney has become "Anonymous." David has become "Blood." Dean joined the fun and became "Clean." Joe thought about calling himself "Joey Diphthong," after his favorite *d* word, but they convinced him to stay as "Jack Talcum," his alter ego (and id) from his imaginative, unhinged bedroom recordings.

Joe was uncertain whether they would remain the Dead Milkmen, but Dean—always handy with a can of spray paint—made up their minds by showing up with his bass drum and fancy cases stenciled "the Dead Milkmen." Dean's younger Pennridge buddy and fellow "drum dork" Jonny Wurster had booked a couple of gigs for them out in Harleysville. The first was their debut show at the youth center in late July, two weeks after Dean joined the band (and a few hours after he'd met Rodney—the band's singer—for the first time). The latter was a fun-as-hell Thanksgiving party at the Wurster home, where they played their whole setlist three times. They'd also landed two geographically diametric gigs in October: one outside an infamous coke-peddling bar on Pine Street in Philthy Philly, and the other in a hayloft in rural Bedminster. The girls who organized that one, including Dean's sister, used their school's art studio to print stickers and T-shirts of a smiling cow with x-ed-out eyes, which Dean (also handy with a Sharpie) had sketched out on a napkin.

On this day in December, the gradually tightening Dead Milkmen are a few days out from their first "real" midnight gig at the East Side Club, opening for a band called 84

Rooms. This isn't Dean's first rodeo, but he's still excited. After causing enough racket to piss off half of Leedom Estates, the band packs it in. Though he'd helped with most of their arrangements, Dean works up the courage to speak, and produces a sheet of notebook paper: "So, I had a crazy dream, and when I woke up, I wrote it down." He doesn't know if it can be anything, but he hands it to Joe. Joe doesn't know if it can be anything, either, but over the holidays he's going to mess with it.

Back in Wagontown, Joe pulls out the notebook page with Dean's dream on it. Inspired by his brother's U2 album, he strums the same chord over and over. "Friday night, cooking show with a horsemeat dish . . ." The result is droning and repetitive, and has no chorus, but who cares? "I escape to a theater to see a girl, with long blond hair . . ." He had turned Dean's dream into "Dean's Dream," and he is excited to bring it back to the band.

For the Dead Milkmen, as the year of Orwell approaches, the world seems just as scary and confusing as advertised. Dean is finally about to move to the big city, leaving his nest in Sellersville. Rodney's been drinking too much, wondering whether it's worth staying in college. Joe is preparing to graduate from college into Reagan's America, where millions cheer on a plague against people like him. And David's already tired of thinking about death.

But in this America, there was the republic of the Dead Milkmen. It may be Dean's dream, but it's Joe's too, and Rodney's, and David's, and a whole bunch of nerds who are going to join the resistance: "He hits me in the back, but I'm alright, I'm alriiiiiight, I'm all riiiiiiight."

He's alright.

Dean, Joe, Dave, and Rodney at the East Side Club in Philadelphia, July 3, 1984. Photo by Scott Dodderer, courtesy of Kurt Schulthise.

1. "PRISONER'S CINEMA"
THE DEAD MILKMEN VS. CAPITALISM

Groucho: Now, what is it that has four pair of pants, lives in Philadelphia, and it never rains, but it pours?
Chico: That's a good one! I'll give ya three guesses . . .
Groucho: Now, let me see . . . is it male or female?
Chico: I don't think so.
Groucho: Is he dead?
Chico: Who?
Groucho: I don't know. I give up!
—Scene from *Duck Soup* (1933)

Both as band and world-building concept, the Dead Milkmen do everything possible to avoid a linear story. Their catalog—eleven LPs (as of this writing), a generous assortment of singles (increasingly self-released), and a deep assortment of well-curated bootlegs—is *a bottomless pit*, a smorgasbord of the last sixty years of Western popular culture. They are likely the only band to open for Odd Future *and* 2 Live Crew. The City of Brotherly Love congealed them, and a heady mix of music industry and interpersonal forces dissolved them in time for the internet to play games with their legacy. After the tragic loss of a founding member, they eventually came back to life, motivated by the disappearance of what brought them down and the ascension of a whole new universe of bullshit. Call what they do a productive iconoclasm, one that celebrates the garbage that brings people together. It's the killer bass intros. It's an orgy. It's scatological humor. It's making people shake their heads in disbelief. It's Charles Nelson Reilly. And that's all just *one* song.

The Dead Milkmen could only have come out of the time they did in the place they did. They were too young to experience Beatlemania along with the boomers, and slightly too old to fully grasp (or tolerate) the nihilism of Generation X. They came of age during "peak terrible," when the promise of the progressive era had given way to the cosmic selfishness of the post-Vietnam malaise and, even worse, "morning in America."

"I think it's really important [to understand] that the Dead Milkmen were a group of working-class guys that went to college," said Stewart Frescas, a chemist, industrial whistleblower, and longtime friend of the band. "And then they saw that their compatriots [and] the people in their families were getting the raw deal and that left them very angry. But they are also very intelligent. They were channeling their anger, which they very much felt, but they were also [thinking] 'What's the most effective way to accomplish this goal?'"

One of the most prescient early observations about the band came from, of all places, Dayton entertainment reporter Mike Conway in a March 1986 "Noises in the Night" segment: "From what I've said so far, you might think I can't stand the Dead Milkmen, but on the contrary, I like them. Believe it or not, not everybody in this generation is studying to be an accountant. Some are angry, and the Milkmen use satire to convey that anger."

"These Generation X authors are missing the point," Rodney Anonymous told the *Daily Illini* in 1994. "The stuff they are writing about has already been done in the 12th and 13th centuries. A large percentage of the population was illiterate, and there was a plague killing everyone."

A more appropriate name for their micro-generation, born between 1955 and 1965, would be the "Bastards of Young." The author of that Replacements song, Paul Westerberg, happened to be born exactly in the middle of that ten-year span. Though the 'Mats have coffee-table books, luxury reissue box sets, and the esteem of the entire graying rock establishment, the Milkmen were, allegedly, outearning them for a stretch of the eighties. Dean Clean even stepped in for Slim Dunlap for an impromptu photo shoot at the Tower Theater in 1987, joining the Replacements (technically) for a few minutes.

Earlier that year, the Milkmen visited Tiger Stadium to say hello to their biggest pro-athlete fan, Jim Walewander. Their appearance curried a write-up in the *Detroit Free Press* by Mitch *Tuesdays with Morrie* Albom. Here is how he imagined their interaction with manager Sparky Anderson:

PR MAN: Sparky, meet the Dead Milkmen.
SPARKY: Well, hello, boys.
MILKMEN: DEATH TO CAPITALISTS!
SPARKY: Well, gotta go, boys.

Not that I would associate Mitch Albom with "punk" any more than humorists associated the Dead Milkmen with "effective," but it's a flattering tableau. Albom quickly admitted the truth: Sparky looked at Dave Blood's earring, camo shirt, and combat boots and said, "Son, don't take no prisoners." The Tigers won that day; Jim Walewander, who had seen the Milkmen the previous night at Paycheck's in Hamtramck, slugged his only Major League home run in the sixth inning. Thirty-six years later, the Dead Milkmen came back to Hamtramck to play a free, very effective Labor Day festival set.

Also, Dave Blood never did take any prisoners. He also never replaced those combat boots. David Schulthise was a true radical, but he held an economics degree and was the band's biggest adherent to the functionality of capitalism. To subvert any system, you had to be willing to work within it. You had to give the people what they wanted.

"We don't pretend that we're important," he told *Spin* in 1990. "We're serious about not being serious. Meaning that we're serious about putting the songs together. We're not a 'cause' band. People plunk down a lot of money to see our shows. Their parents are giving them shit, their teachers are giving them shit, they're worried about drugs, AIDS, herpes and shit. They just want to have a great time. . . . Last night I was involved in an important process that made 300 people really happy—and another 100 want their money back."

It's fitting that the city that birthed America, and which is *still* doing the heavy lifting to keep the Republic together, also birthed the Dead Milkmen. The Milkmen all grew up in working-class families on her periphery as the "methamphetamine capital of the East Coast" cranked out *Rocky*, Frank Rizzo's reign of terror, some of the greatest soul music ever put to tape, multiple serial killers—two of whom allegedly saw the Dead Milkmen play at Abe's Steaks in 1985—and at least one mass murderer.

"Philadelphia is cool," Rodney Anonymous told *Rock Express* in 1987. "You can sell millions and they'll still treat you like scum there!" Twenty years later, he was writing columns for the Philadelphia *City Paper*, celebrating his adopted hometown's "more sarcastic smartasses per square foot than any other city in the world. The dumbest Philadelphian is still twice as smart as the average New Yorker and ten times brighter than anyone in Alabama."

"There must be something in the wooder [*sic*]," wrote drummer and comedian Jon Wurster. "Philly is such a weird mix of people and world views. It's working class, but there's a lot of higher education and 'fancy people,' too. It really is a perfect melting pot of high class and trash, and that all adds to the weirdness of the city."

"Philadelphia's a great town to fuck up in," laughs Chris Coccia, a comedian and early collaborator of the Dead Milkmen, "because you're flying under the radar, right? It allows you to mess around . . . I heard somebody say that, I wish I could credit them."

"It's a weird city," says nerdcore rapper MC Lars (alias Andrew Nielsen), who relocated to the area. "Everyone's like 'keep Portland weird,' 'keep Austin weird'—that's always the model, but Philly is actually weird. You don't have to keep it weird. It always was."

"I think the Dead Milkmen could not have come from anywhere else besides Philly," says Froggy bassist Brooke Feenie. "There is a raw realness to Philadelphia, a scrappy, self-made, honesty about it, that I think the Dead Milkmen have always exhibited. I think they came from the perfect place at the perfect time, and it's easy to feel connected to them when you're in Philadelphia."

"A lot of the people in Philadelphia generally felt kind

of bad about Philadelphia," reflects recording engineer Brian McTear, who moved in from the Lehigh Valley in the nineties. "They didn't necessarily want you. [Take] Gritty, the Flyers mascot. People initially didn't like Gritty. And then, the moment some person from outside of Philadelphia made a negative comment about Gritty, everybody in Philly was like, *Fuck you, man, he's ours!*"

Though Gritty wouldn't emerge until 2018, his genesis could arguably be traced to fall 2008. On October 11, the Flyers hosted the New York Rangers in their home opener, and the NHL agreed to let Sarah Palin, the canary in the Trumpism coal mine, do the ceremonial puck drop to abet the Republican branding of her as "America's hockey mom." Scott Gomez, the Rangers' captain and longtime Jersey Devil, was the league's biggest Alaska-bred star. Gomez and Flyers' captain Mike Richards sidled up to the face-off circle as the inevitable happened: a cacophony of boos, middle fingers, and a bunch of Obama-Biden posters the TV cameras worked diligently to conceal. Who the hell thought this would be a good idea?

Two weeks later, on the heels of Obama's impending election victory and the ensuing age of reactionary unreason, the Dead Milkmen played a secret gig at Johnny Brenda's in fast-gentrifying Fishtown. They opened their set with a clip of Palin gratingly declaring: "I had the privilege of living most of my life in a small town." Joe Jack Talcum ripped that familiar E-major 7th chord (the one he chose to prove to the Electric Love Muffin's Rich Kaufmann that he could) and the band launched into "Tiny Town." Over twenty years since it purposefully and offensively led off their first record, it felt even more relevant. At another warm-up gig, Rodney devoted his monologue during the loungey intro to

"Bitchin' Camaro" to the importance of local elections in a time of unprecedented liberal fervor over the federal one. Obama's victory would mean nothing when motherfuckers who believed the world was six thousand years old still sat on school boards.

Humor, replete with a Borscht Belt flavor, as much as power chords and catchy hooks, was what separated the Dictators and the Ramones from bloated arena rock in 1975. People were not ready for the seething satire of the former's "Master Race Rock" at the time. The same could be said for "Tiny Town" in 1985, an era of (to borrow from Harlan Ellison) "hyperthyroid provincialism." Both the album and single "Born in the USA" were flying off shelves, making Bruce Springsteen the biggest star to emerge from "down the shore." John Cougar Mellencamp (whose surname Rodney would append to his stage name in 1986) scored a string of hits romanticizing small-town Indiana—a landscape with which Dave Blood was awfully familiar. "Tiny Town" was a perfect opening track to the official Dead Milkmen discography, throwing down the gauntlet against the monocultural humbug of Heartland Rock while eternally dunking on liberalism.

"We got a letter from a radio station saying [they banned 'Tiny Town']," Rodney recalled. "They were this ultra-liberal station that was against censorship. I was so confused that they couldn't see it was a parody, so I explained 'parody' to them, and they were like, *Thank you for explaining that, but you're still banned.'* Sometimes it's a badge of honor to be banned by certain people."

Thirty-eight years later, they would open their eleventh album *Quaker City Quiet Pills* with an echoing sentiment on "Grandpa's Not a Racist (He Just Voted for One)." Both conveyed uncomfortable truths about the racism embedded in American life, wrapped in satire befitting Abbie Hoffman, Randy Newman, or Kinky Friedman (with whom the Milkmen partied at least once). It was a purposefully difficult pill to swallow, back then as it remains today.

"At that point, my sarcasm detectors were not as refined," said "Atom" Goren (alias Atom and His Package), who covered "Nutrition" in 1997 and played a Ramones cover set with Rodney in 2010. "I remember being a little bit troubled-slash-puzzled by 'Tiny Town' and its lyrics, in the context of the rest of [their songs, where] they were good-hearted and funny. I remember hearing 'Tiny Town' for the first time, and I was like, *Wait, what? They don't hate Blacks! They don't hate Jews!* It's just funny—as a little kid, you don't know what's happening, ever."

"'Tiny Town' was just such a huge, relatable song to me," said Raws Schlesinger, founder of "America's Leather Band," Plack Blague. "Growing up as a gay kid in the middle of nowhere, I felt like that song was about me in a lot of ways. I related to that song so much because there was so much racism, so much homophobia around where I live . . . I just related to being different. It encapsulates everything about my upbringing. It's just a huge 'Fuck you,' and I love that about it."

"Exurban and rural kids kind of got what they were doing a lot more than people in the city or even, like, near suburbs," says Philly hardcore veteran Chuck Meehan. "I know they connected with these people who grew up in the country towns or small towns. And maybe that's why they did so well at rural colleges, these small-town colleges."

Considering how strongly the Dead Milkmen wore Philly on their sleeves, they did build a substantial rural fan base. It makes sense. Joe Jack Talcum, who started the project, grew up as a gay kid living in rural America. Rodney Anonymous and Dean Clean also grew up provincially, and Dave Blood spent much of his young life (and last years of his life) choked by suburbia.

In 2015, the Dead Milkmen gathered at Miner Street to record an exclusive single for Weathervane Music, a nonprofit cofounded by McTear. Thirty years since "Tiny Town" and five years into their second chapter, the most successful export of Philadelphia hardcore had arrived at what Rodney termed "folk-punk-triphop-industrial." To continue getting their music into the world and "accomplishing this goal," they needed trusted collaborators. McTear and his partner Amy Morrissey, among their most trusted, put it bluntly: "When you try to straighten out the Dead Milkmen, they cease to be the Dead Milkmen."

"Prisoner's Cinema" begins with guest vocalist Jill Knapp, whom Rodney recruited because "she has a beautiful voice, and I don't," chanting us into the song like Chumbawamba stoned in the Mummers Parade. And then it gets unsettling. Rodney declares that "no one writes songs about the poor anymore," slams the Wobblies songbook on the table, admonishing corporate America for stripping back benefits and wages "'til you're nearly working for free." As their old comrades the Minutemen said, to "put it in simple worlds, working men [or however they choose to identify] are pissed."

Considering how attached the Dead Milkmen are to the Reagan era in public memory, "Prisoner's Cinema" was a rallying cry in the dying embers of the Obama era. Liberal optimism was getting a wake-up call: citizens were turning their cars into taxis and their spare bedrooms into hotels, and figuring out clever new ways to stick their hands into each other's pockets. While taking swipes at office culture, the song calls attention to the closest thing America still has to a working class: people who wake up at 3 a.m., thousands of miles from their families, to spray Eagles fans' puke (and whatever horseshit the fans didn't ingest) off the street before the suit-and-tie crowd files in. For Dandrew Stevens, piloting the track with his bass line, it's the ones who worked hard to raise three kids, got fired from their jobs during COVID, and had to DoorDash to make ends meet, getting nickel-and-dimed by our tech overlords. All his bandmates have these stories.

Rodney's anger was fully realized in Philly, but it was bred in Coatesville, the home of Lukens Steel, where his father worked as a foreman for over forty years. His father's career traversed the rise of unions and the decimation of the industry by cheap Japanese imports in the seventies. In 1956, Rodney P. Linderman graduated from Scott Senior High School along with his progressive (and talkative) sweetheart Mary Work, and they married the next year. They would often ride into the city to Studio B at Forty-Sixth and Market, where they would dance on *American Bandstand* as it first went national on ABC. An early iteration of the Dead Milkmen would romanticize this, Ray Davies–style, in "On Bandstand" in 1982. The Lindermans' experience placed them on the front lines of the rise of teen idols like South Philadelphia's Frankie Avalon (born Francis Avallone). In 1970, Frankie Avalon cohosted the "Our Little Miss" child beauty pageant on CBS, earning a severe excoriation from Harlan Ellison. In 1986, his character would appear in the Dead Milkmen's "Beach Party Vietnam" with his arms blown off.

"To me, our music is very sad or very angry with little bits of humor slipped in to make it palatable," Rodney told *PennLive*. "It's like the Porter's speech in *Macbeth*. Here's a whole play about regicide but, in the middle of it, there's a guy complaining about his job."

At FYF Fest in Los Angeles in 2011, Rodney devoted his "Bitchin' Camaro" spiel to blaming Michele and Marcus "pray away the gay" Bachmann for over a dozen LGBT teen suicides in her Minnesota district that year. He suggested that the lawmaker's iron-closeted husband was a big South Carolina Gamecocks fan, leading the crowd in a chant of "MARCUS BACHMANN LOVES THOSE COCKS! MARCUS BACHMANN LOVES THOSE COCKS!"

The Dead Milkmen spent a lifetime getting labeled as something tantamount to "punk's comedy troupe." Given enough space, I could add a full appendix of bad headlines like: "Philadelphia's Pre-Eminent Punk Rock Pranksters," "Some Milk and Kookies," "Milkmen Pour on the Satire," "Milkmen's Delivery Is Curdled," "Moo to You," and the most 1992-coded headline ever printed: "Delivering Serious Songs . . . Not!" The Dead Milkmen and their "comical" indie counterparts (e.g., New York's King Missile, Melbourne's This Is Serious Mum, a.k.a. T.I.S.M.) were undervalued because comedy has a bad habit of being undervalued in its time. The Marx Brothers and Three Stooges—both household names that transcended vaudeville, conquered the silver screen, and enjoyed careers that spanned half a century— never got validation from the critical establishment until it was too late. Despite having two films now preserved in the National Film Registry (1933's *Duck Soup* and 1935's

A Night at the Opera), the Marx Brothers never garnered a major Oscar nomination. The Three Stooges, starring Philadelphia-native Louis Feinberg (better known as Larry Fine), got one nomination for their anarchic two-reeler *Men in Black* (1934) but never got one raise from Columbia. Today, nobody cares who won that Oscar, but a giant mural of Larry and his violin towers over his birthplace by Third and South, blocks from where Zipperhead, the Philadelphia Pizza Company, and a beleaguered Blockbuster Video once stood.

By being "serious about not being serious," the Milkmen were, ironically, to the left of so many urbane punk bands. In many respects, the Dead Milkmen are the quintessential punk-nerd group, beloved by a list of celebrity fans including *Simpsons* creator Matt Groening, *Dungeons & Dragons* pilot Ray Winninger, and actor Wil Wheaton, who wrote a testimonial for the *Now We Are 20* retrospective in 2003. In 2025, though the band had little to do with it, their mascot-logo appeared prominently on Chris Pratt's T-shirt and truck in *The Electric State*, a $320 million boondoggle for Netflix. The Milkmen remain the most common go-to reference in a review of any band who dares mix punk with humor.

This prompts a greater question of punk: Where *was* this cabal of humorless fucks who ran things in the eighties? The Ramones were still touring and singing about falling in love at the Burger King. Adrenalin O.D., whose song "Trans Am" allegedly inspired "Bitchin' Camaro" (according to *Going Underground* author George Hurchalla), were playing all the time in New Jersey. Even the Minor Threat kids—later revealed via Dischord box set studio cutouts—could be cutups. Punk was *supposed* to be funny. The Misfits, whom the Milkmen loved, emerged from suburban New Jersey and sang about "Teenagers from Mars" and something called "Astro Zombies."

"Glenn Danzig was actually a very funny young man before he became the world's most gigantic butthole!" exclaimed Tesco Vee on a 2019 panel seated next to dry, witty former Minor Threat drummer Jeff Nelson. Tesco's Meatmen, like their Michigander contemporaries the Crucifucks, simultaneously raised and lowered the bar for anarchist irreverence in hardcore. The Milkmen would parody his "Meatmen Stomp" as the "Milkmen Stomp" in their 1984 *Sellersville Sessions*—a demo recorded in Dean's parents' basement with an audience of friends and siblings. It was a catalog of their corner of the Philadelphia hardcore scene, ultimately exposing Flag of Democracy (F.O.D.), Little Gentlemen, YDI, and others to the world outside the Commonwealth. All these bands were, variably, hilarious.

"The Dead Milkmen did, actually [play with the Dickies], and they're not serious!" Joe Genaro told *Cheap Shot Philly* in 2008. "And the Angry Samoans, and they're not serious. And the Minutemen actually have their humor."

The Minutemen absolutely had their humor, taking it so far as to cover their van's back window with a poster of the Three Stooges. In 2010, I asked Mike Watt which Stooge was his favorite.

"I don't know," he pondered, "Moe always played the Stalinist. But . . . those guys needed each other."

If Boon, Watt, and Hurley were punk's Howard, Fine, and Howard, then the Dead Milkmen are unquestionably its Marx Brothers. Rodney is Groucho, the Borscht Belt anarchist wiseass who talked circles around everyone (though his father would become more famous for posing with a cigar, on the cover of *Beelzebubba*). Joe Jack Talcum is Harpo: the quiet, expressive one—an inveterate collector who is good with strings and always in cahoots with somebody. Dave Blood was Chico, the fearless elder statesman who could talk his way into or out of anything, skilled with women and silly accents. Dean Clean is Zeppo: the multitalented "normal" one who pays their taxes and could play the straight man when absolutely necessary. Reagan's (and then Bush's, and then Clinton's, etc.) America has always been their Margaret Dumont, that wealthy dowager at the butt of their jokes who had no idea what was going on. As if to drive this home, they covered "Lydia, the Tattooed Lady" on Dr. Demento's 2018 Covered in Punk compilation. *Hail, Philly, and hail, Freedonia!*

In 1988, Dave Blood explained his "theory of salad dynamics" to *Creem* magazine: "Rodney has no salad. I have a plain salad. Dean has Italian dressing and Joe Jack has Thousand Island. Now do you get it?"

Typical of many Blood-lines, he was simultaneously pulling the interviewer's leg while making a point: The Dead Milkmen have always been four very different people, with four distinct working-class family backgrounds, four different musical pedigrees, four *quite* different personalities, and even four different manners of messing with journalists, record labels, zinesters, and possibly even this author. The handful of values that do overlap include honesty, an antipathy for rock star bullshit, and an inability to stop creating music. Listing the other bands and collaborations of the individual Milkmen would take half a page. To expand the list into solo projects would fill a whole page.

"We are all very different, but I think that everybody in the group appreciates that fact because, in reality, that was the strength of our relationship," David wrote in his final interview in 2003. "We all brought different things to the process. Some people might call it synergy. Maybe that's what it is, but it worked well for us right up until the end of the band thing. It never got ugly, although it got a bit strange at times."

2. *MUSIC FOR THE MINDLESS*
THE DEAD MILKMEN VS. BOREDOM

The cassette is the counterculture's most dangerous and subversive weapon. It is a threat, an incendiary device, the perfect tool for the cultural anarchist . . . cassettes truly are the most democratic art form!
—Robin James in *Cassette Mythos* (1992)

Shortly after three-quarters of the Dead Milkmen were born, the Philips company released the compact cassette. As they grew up, especially for Joe Genaro, tapes transformed the way kids conquered boredom endemic to the suburbs. In the privacy of their bedrooms, a generation of young suburbanites pressed "Record" and proceeded to say the dumbest thing imaginable. It may not have been "funny" or "listenable," but in their moment of creation, they refracted the shows we were watching, the music we were listening to, and whatever we needed to say to crack up whoever was sitting next to us. In western Massachusetts in the early nineties, my cousin, friends, and I created a "radio show" called *The Drawer Connection*. It posited a bizarre world where characters like the geriatric Mrs. Pumpernickel called in, unsure of where she was. We promised to force-feed Maalox to our lucky two-hundredth caller. Characters would loudly interject, apropos of nothing, "PENIS!" We've long since grown up and our senses of humor have matured, but in that moment when we were twelve, it was the funniest shit in the world.

The Dead Milkmen, in their ongoing existence, serve as validation for that generation of bored creatives armed with blank cassette tapes. Like attempting to pinpoint the "big bang" of punk rock, divining *the moment* the Dead Milkmen began is a fool's errand. The band started as a world-building project in the mind of bored teenagers living at the interface of steel town and Amish country. If any moment forged the girders or raised the barn, though, it was October 15, 1972, when Tony and Betty Genaro gifted Joey a portable Lloyd personal cassette recorder for his tenth birthday.

"It didn't have a built-in microphone like the later models would," Genaro recalls, "but it came with a microphone that had a little eighth-inch jack. And that was when my love of recording started. I brought it everywhere."

Genaro's stab at cassette comedy came in the form of "the Jerrock Jerks," a duo with his neighbor Garth Scott. As Joe remembers it, the name originated as a mash-up of their last names and was mangled into "jer-rock" because it sounded better. Garth played "Pope Garth O'Neil," while Joe, after glancing at a bottle of talcum powder from the toilet one day, brewed up a character named Jack Talcum. Years later, its "softness" would provide a perfect contrarian stage name to the glass-eating hardcore scene, but in that moment he just liked how it sounded. The Jerrock Jerks would record a "show," listen back and laugh their asses off, and then tape over it. By 1974, Joey began messing around with "high-performance" pseudo-chrome tapes that enabled rerecording with minimal loss of quality. Soon, Joe discovered primitive methods for overdubs and other adolescent audio experiments.

"My method of 'multi-track' recording back then involved playing back the original base recording from one cassette deck into another deck which had a line-in and a microphone-in which could be mixed," Joe told the *Tapewrecks* blog in 2013. "That mixed signal would be recorded as the overdubbed track. If I wanted more overdubs, I repeated the process. Most of the in-between takes would be dubbed over to save tape."

His cassette/culture jamming leveled up on his fifteenth birthday, when his parents gave him his first guitar. Fuel came from a steady supply of jukebox singles retired from his uncle's restaurant in Coatesville. The first happened to be the Beatles' "Hello, Goodbye" backed with "I Am the Walrus" (a title the Milkmen would steal in 1987), igniting a lifelong love affair with the Fab Four and "the sixties." Despondent that he'd missed the Beatles by a few years, Joe joined the Wings Fun Club, which produced a UK-based Paul McCartney fanzine. The newsletter was produced by mononymous young women called Claire, Lucy, and Nicky. The first five issues were crudely designed and mimeographed, offering a heady mix of fawning or critical fan letters along with tabloid accounts of goings-on in Paul's life. Joe listened to Dylan, the Byrds, and the Beatles around the clock, learning to play along, dreaming of folk-rock stardom. When punk rock seeped into Coatesville, he added the Ramones to the soundtrack and imagined what folk-punk stardom would be like. He recognized and appreciated the humor in what they did.

"For me," said Genaro, "the first inkling that I had that songs could be funny came from listening to the Dr. Demento radio show when I was a kid. Also, I loved *Monty Python's Flying Circus*. I would watch it with my mom on the local public TV station. They used music a lot, and their songs were also played on the Dr. Demento show, and I would later buy some of their albums."

New experiments in sketch comedy like *Saturday Night Live* and *Second City Television* (SCTV) also had an incalculable influence on Joe and his future bandmates. An hour northeast in Perkasie, Dean Sabatino and his friend Steve Wallis cowrote and costarred in *The Sab & Wally Show*, a "program of comedy and entertainment" on Channel 8 on Pennridge Cable TV. Sabatino had been born in Camden, New Jersey—a post-post-industrial suburb of Philly known for the world's first drive-in theater (1933) and for multiple generations of economic free fall. Dean's folks, educators William and Beth, moved him up to Sellersville, where Dean's sister Nina was born five years later. Though he wasn't the only Dead Milkman to come from a musical family, his pedigree ran deep. His grandfather, Ward Bynum, grew up in Alabama, playing guitar in jazz bands like Billy Stewart's Orchestra before chasing wartime work to Delaware. Dean retains fond childhood memories of attending bluegrass festivals with his grandpa, as much as he admits being too young to recognize any of the legendary thumb pickers.

After the Sabatinos spent the 1972–73 academic year in England, Dean returned with a head full of prog-rock and grand ambitions for his drum kit. He had a rare opportunity to attend a drum clinic taught by legally blind Joe Morello, whose virtuosic work on Dave Brubeck's *Time Out* had long soundtracked the Sabatino household. At Pennridge High

School, Dean maintained star-student status, ran track, starred in a summer-theater production of "The Good Doctor," and contributed to several public-art projects. By his senior year, he became director of the Pennridge Student Band (whose members would appear in his dreams for years afterward). Though *Sab & Wally* was a footnote among his extracurricular accomplishments, he would importantly gain production assistance from a former jock named David Reckner.

Meanwhile in Caln, closer to Wagontown, Rodney Linderman was growing up, and becoming, television. Months after Rodney's birth on May 21, 1963 (exactly one year after Dean), Allan Sherman's *My Son, the Nut* topped the *Billboard* charts—the last comedy/novelty record to do so for more than fifty years. His kitschy, nebbishy tunes were mainstays of the Linderman household, along with dirty parodies his folks would sing of the theme to *The Waltons.* Rodney's lifelong appreciation of Rodney Dangerfield would give fans (who didn't know his goyish surname) the understandable impression that he was Jewish. By 1983, he was peppering his correspondence with "oy vey." By 1993, he was peppering songs like "I Dream of Jesus" with references to Manischewitz bottles. In December 2025, Rodney joined an all-star lineup (which included Laurie Anderson, Robert Smigel, and the Hooters' Eric Bazilian) in a tribute to Sherman at the Weitzman National Museum of American Jewish History. He sang the Dr. Seuss–penned "I'm a Punk," as performed by Sherman as the *Cat in the Hat* on CBS in 1971—a pivotal year in his TV-drenched childhood.

Also in 1971, young Rodney made another pivotal discovery on one of the Linderman family's beach trips.

Wandering with his father's metal detector, eight-year-old Rodney experienced what felt like making music for the first time. His father played the accordion, and his folks had bought him a drum kit when he was five (he busted them open to see what was inside), but *this* was the instrument for him. He never wearied in his devotion to open-access noise. Rodney maintains that "his instrument" is the computer over anything else. "I'm oddly musical for someone who can't play for shit," he told *Razorcake* in 2009.

On the road with the Dead Milkmen, Rodney would keep his hotel TV on from check-in until checkout. Following a pivotal visit to Graceland in October 1986, he nearly threw a fit at the prospect of missing the annual CBS broadcast of *It's the Great Pumpkin, Charlie Brown*. The Milkmen detoured to a department store in some mall outside Little Rock to get him his fix. From his earliest zine interviews, he spoke brazenly of his reverence for Charles Nelson Reilly. "He's so cool," he told one. "He doesn't have books or movies, but he's always on Carson. We don't even know why he's there." If there *was* a god—they baptized their son a Methodist, but the Lindermans were wholly secular—it may as well have been America's favorite confirmed bachelor. Years after Reilly's death in 2007, the Milkmen are almost single-handedly responsible for anyone under fifty knowing who he was—possibly Bob Crane and Steve McGarrett (Jack Lord) too. Conversely, Rodney expressed disdain for Reilly's counterparts like Gavin MacLeod and Jerry Lewis, who would, as an early Milkmen song declared, "fuck up their Labor Day" with his annual telethon. Though Lewis remains a household name, the "King of Comedy" did little at the end of his life to dispel long-standing notions that he was an insufferable asshole.

"Not enough musicians watch TV. . . . One episode of *Divorce Court* is worth four or five songs," Rodney told the *Asbury Park Press* in 1989, before admitting he'd learned on *Entertainment Tonight* that Donovan's "Mellow Yellow" was allegedly about inhaling banana-peel fumes. While watching *Wild in the Streets* with his sisters, Rodney was entranced at how Max Frost pulled current events out of newspapers to write songs. Years later, once the Dead Milkmen could leverage a tour rider, they demanded a local newspaper so Rodney knew what regional issues to rant about during "Bitchin' Camaro" or, beginning in 1989, kick back and read during "Punk Rock Girl."

When Rodney began high school in Coatesville, he stopped growing around five foot three and quickly got tired of looking up at his classmates. One of the places he could hold court was sitting down at the lunch table, where he cracked up his fellow diners, including the similarly diminutive sophomore Joe Genaro.

"Rodney was probably the funniest guy in my high school," recalls Joe. "It would be hard to have a conversation with him, even a serious one, without laughing at some point. And his humor made you think. He had a good mind for satire."

Though he and Joe had spent time at the same crowded lunch table for much of that fall, the two hadn't really connected socially. Garth, however, shared a journalism class with Rodney, which made him more confident in handing his chatty classmate a dubbed copy of *So Long, Seventies* by "the Dead Milkmen with Jack Talcum Jr."

●

There are three things the Dead Milkmen have been asked about more than any punk band in history: comedy, Philadelphia, and "So, where'd you come up with your name?" The alternate versions (a.k.a. lies) are usually funny and incredibly dark. In 1985, Rodney told Al Quint of Boston's *Suburban Voice* that he and Joe were in Vietnam, and the guy who took a bullet for them as they escaped on a helicopter made them promise to name the band for his mother: "I'm pretty sure he said Dead Milkmen. He might have said Doors." In a 1989 issue of their own zine, the *DM Newzletter*, they told a fan in the UK that their original manager, a former milk truck driver, had suggested the name Amazing Aardvarks, so they shot him in the head. In June 1990, Dave Blood told John Bonner of *Short Cutz*, among other unflinching fabrications, that the name was a tribute to a milkman named Freddie who died while the Genaros were on vacation.

The most repeated version is that Joe took the name from the protagonist Macon "Milkman" Dead III in Toni Morrison's landmark 1977 novel *Song of Solomon*. Rodney still insists that the Genaros had a copy of the book in 1980. Today, Joe admits it wasn't until around 1986 when a young fan and aspiring music journalist named Richard Abowitz recommended it to him. The Milkmen were all adept at reading in the van, so the book made its way around quickly. Incidentally, Milkman Dead's cousin, who fantasized about "killing whitey," is nicknamed Guitar. In a 1987 interview for the *Still Thinking* zine, Joe said the name came from the book, and the band let that story ride.

The honest version (or so Joe says) is that the "Dead" part came from the "punkest" band he knew of in 1979, the Dead Boys. To a provincial teenager, why wouldn't his fictional band start with an edgy word like "dead"?

"I was actually not aware of the Dead Kennedys yet, though I came to be really jealous of their name," Joe admits.

"Milkmen" came from a term to represent the bucolic countryside. The cows in the pasture across the street. The Amish guy who delivered eggs on his horse and buggy. Until the early seventies, the Genaros had a milkman, but he vanished by the time supermarkets had supplanted the need for dairy delivery. Urban blight had also hollowed cities out to the point that delivering milk door-to-door was risky; rampant gun violence had placed "milkman" among the most-shot-at professions. On September 9, 1981, two North Philly teens shot and killed a thirty-four-year-old milkman named Richard Breves next to his truck. According to an article the following month in the *Inquirer*, Breves worked for Breuninger Dairies "as one of the city's few remaining door-to-door milkmen." Genaro, then in his sophomore year at Temple, shared it with Rodney as a sign about the "Dead Milkmen" project.

The name made a perfect ironic juxtaposition of "punk" and "folk," two genres that, in Joe's world, nobody in their right mind would ever mix. Then again, even as an abstraction in the head of a teenage Joe, the Dead Milkmen were more interesting than 90 percent of the first-wave punk bands they were mocking. Given a steady diet of rock literature, Joe and Garth developed an unhinged backstory for Jack Talcum Sr. and his ungrateful bizarro-Dylan son, Jack Talcum Jr. It would be five years before the Milkmen and their buddy Jonny Wurster would see *This Is Spinal Tap* hit theaters, but Joe imagined a "(Listen to the) Flower People" in the form of the "Sunflower Children of God." In an apocryphal early recording, their keyboardist "Richard

Nixon" (LSD made him forget his real name) keeled over and died, generating a droning hum of his head on the keys in the background.

Inspired by the DIY nature of the Wings Fun Club newsletters, Joe started imagining an evil counterpart. What if the team of agents, producers, and backup musicians who worked for Jack Talcum Jr. openly hated him? What if he and his backup band, the Creeps, toured in places as far-flung as the Congo and then-revolutionary Tehran? What if he just created and quickly killed off characters with names like George Urine, Ray Pickle, and Bernie Wimplebean III? Joe would attempt to record real-life versions of fictional advertised albums like *Country Sh!t and Other Garbage*. Typing fictional letters to the fictional editor (who happened to be Jack Talcum) on his family typewriter, Joe would cut and paste them together with whatever photos Garth would hand him, scribbling notes and toons in the margins à la *MAD* magazine.

This was all the by-product of supportive families as much as boredom and creativity. The Genaros and Scotts would entertain their adolescent sons' dice game concepts. One game Joe devised was inspired by the fifties radio payola scandal (a lifelong preoccupation, as nodded to in "Methodist Coloring Book"). He and Garth wondered what a payola board game would be like, borrowing components like a spinner from other games, and fighting their way up and down imaginary *Billboard* charts. Their brain synapses fired off a new fictional song or, ultimately, a new element of the Jack Talcum legend with every roll or spin.

"I think the biggest fault was that the game really didn't have an ending," said Joe.

Though he had been culture-jamming on cassette for a

couple of years, the first official (unofficial) Dead Milkmen tape was recorded on December 31, 1979. Joe, Garth, and some family friends spent the Genaro New Year's Eve party huddled in front of the tape recorder, offering scattered improvisations, laughing between takes as Joe recorded overdubs. They dubbed a couple copies for friends, not that anybody in the world outside Coatesville would ever hear it.

"Here's a thought that'll keep you up at night," said Rodney. "I listened to [*So Long, Seventies*] and said, 'Yes, I would, indeed, like to commit several decades of my life to this project.'"

Back at school that January, moments before Joe's bus arrived, Rodney ran over to him, saying he wanted in on the next recording session. He had a banjo he thought would be good to add to the mix. Joe had never thought of what he and Garth did as "recording sessions," but he said sure. Among the first results was "Mr. Radioman," a three-way cacophony between Jack Talcum, Pope Garth, and "Jake Jiles," a belligerent banjo-plucking hayseed. The song was a centerpiece on *Folk Songs for the 80's*. It was a mess. It was irreverent. It was the Dead Milkmen.

Thirty years later, the Dead Milkmen issued a series of seven-inch singles. One, "Big Words Make the Baby Jesus Cry," included artwork they'd hand-stamped. Joe printed and cut the download cards at home, which was a pain in the ass, but that's DIY. In 1985, Rodney sang on "Swordfish," "Why should we buy postage stamps? We can make our own!" Thirty years later, the Dead Milkmen had come full circle. The artwork for another single, "The Great Boston Molasses Flood," was a fabricated 1919-style newspaper that would have been at home in the *DM Newzletter* (though it was made with convenient digital software). It featured an archival photo of the sweet and sticky deluge on the front, and a photo of "Edyth D'Ascoyne"—Dave Blood in drag—on the back. Even success in the music industry, nearly fifteen years of hiatus, and the tragic loss of a pillar member hadn't dislodged the band's spirit of world-building.

The B-side to "Molasses Flood" was called "Now I Wanna Hold Your Dog," inspired by "Wild" Bill Fergusson, Rodney's friend and erstwhile late-nineties bandmate in Burn Witch Burn, who would aggressively compliment rich people's purebred dogs. It's ninety seconds of feedback and distortion-filled mayhem with the call-and-response "Some call it class warfare, but I CALL IT LOVE!" "Now I Wanna Hold Your Dog" concludes, following an obscure Ringo Starr quote, with Rodney Anonymous—well-read, happily married, gainfully employed, and months shy of his fiftieth birthday—screaming at the top of his lungs: "PENIS!!!!"

It's the funniest shit in the world.

3. "WATCHING SCOTTY DIE" THE DEAD MILKMEN VS. THE SUBURBS

I've gone mad and I'm foaming at the mouth. Garth works at Kmart. Life is shit. Come home quick. Curl Sagen [sic] *is not God. Jack Talcum is not Carl Sagen . . .*
—Excerpt of a letter from Rodney to Joe, circa 1981

As Joe approached graduation in 1980, he was vacillating between music and television, leaning toward the latter. His first choice for college was Boston University, which accepted him into their Communications program. However, the out-of-state costs to someone of his means would have meant substantial loans from the expanding predatory program. Meanwhile, nearby Temple had a good Radio-TV-Film (RTF) program, and they offered him enough grants so that his loans could be meager enough for the Dead Milkmen to eventually pay off.

By his sophomore year, Genaro was getting better at working up the courage to engage with strangers sporting cool patches and T-shirts. He spotted one such stranger, decked out from head to toe, moving an awesome crate of records on the elevator. Joe didn't speak up at first, but this new guy—with his prominent mohawk—was easy to spot in the cafeteria. Genaro approached this true-blue punk, who also happened to be named Joe. They anointed their friendship with the inevitable sharing of cool and obscure bands. Joe Schulthise wowed Joe Genaro with stories of Dow Jones and the Industrials and the Zero Boys from Indiana. Genaro eventually admitted that he and his friends had a band (sort of), and that he was looking for a bassist.

Shortly after the spring semester began, Schulthise brought his older brother David to Genaro's dorm room. The elder Schulthise came wielding a bass and, still drinking heavily, produced a smuggled bottle of gin. Genaro wasn't a big drinker, but he accepted a few shots. David shared stories of his life with Joe over their first few jam sessions. They were both the oldest of four kids and named for their respective fathers—Joe's real first name was Anthony, though he was always "Joey." David's folks' only planned child was his sister Kathleen, who was two years younger. His brothers, Joe and Kurt, came along as "Irish twins" in 1962 and 1963. Somewhere in the middle, his loving mother, Margie, had at least one miscarriage—he and his brothers were convinced it had something to do with all the toxic crap in Ridley Park. Maybe it was the nearby coal-fired power plant that rained ashes over Leedom Estates— the same thing he was convinced gave him deadly asthma. His worst attack happened on the day of his high school graduation party; his dad sped him to the emergency room, where they overloaded him with prednisone, likely fucking up his immune system. David got sick *all* the time.

His middle name came from his maternal grandfather, Martin Lashley, an Irish Catholic—ten kids!—from down the shore near Atlantic City. The old man had lost *everything* during the Depression, and it took a multigenerational toll.

For Dave and his siblings growing up, any type of reckless spending was verboten; their dad would force them all to endure terse "family financial meetings." As Colin Camerer, the UPenn economics professor who would sign their first recording contract, could tell them, this was common among "Depression babies."

Maybe this had something to do with David's inability to follow through with nearly anything. He'd moved out to West Lafayette in 1979 to start a PhD in economics at Purdue but hated it, so he quit and worked as a night janitor. His group of friends were smart people who cared about public health, given the horrendous shit these corporations were doing to the environment. Thank God for the EPA. One of his friends, Stewart, who worked for Great Lakes Chemical, was living for *free* in some trashy trailer park because he managed it. They got drunk all the time and went to see Dow Jones and the Industrials play at the Family Inn, a rotten banquet hall.

In May 1980, after David spent half a year scrubbing toilets and getting drunk, his brother Joe came out with a bass guitar he'd bought off their neighbor. They both got jobs at Von's, a greasy, hippie diner that aggravated *both* their allergies. In the interim, David had tried to start a band with his friend Sheila on vocals, but she wasn't into it. He found this redheaded townie named Danny who drove a Camaro to jam with, but they couldn't land a drummer. When it was time for his brother to start at Temple, David decided to move back to Philly with him. They loaded up his puke-green '68 Impala—which their crew all called the "ghetto cruiser"—and putt-putted their way back across Ohio and Pennsylvania. The Impala wasn't long for this world, and David, being excessively frugal, loving "the sauce," and of poor peripheral vision—a nurse had slipped and stabbed his eye with forceps within moments of his birth—would never own another car.

Joe told Dave about his obsession with "the sixties," especially Bob Dylan. He also had a subscription to *Mother Jones* magazine in high school, so he was angry about the environment and this Reagan guy too. His folks had both been teachers at King's Highway Elementary, though his mom quit when he was born in 1962 to take care of him and his three younger siblings. David impressed Joe with a panoply of classic rock knowledge, including his abiding love of Mott the Hoople and the truth bomb that the Sweet's "Little Willy" was, in fact, about an erection. Genaro, lacking elder siblings, was in awe of jamming with someone who had actually *experienced* Beatlemania. His admiration ran deep.

Within a session or two, Genaro and Schulthise coauthored a Ramones rip-off called "I Don't Wanna." Joe was also slowly realizing that, after two years of student loans, books, and dorms at Temple, this was what he really wanted to do. Desperate to escape dorm life, Genaro accepted an invitation to move to a house David and his Hoosier buddy Danny had found over at 4445 Baker Street in Manayunk. Unfortunately, the house wouldn't be open until September. He feared losing his job at the Temple University library, so he found a room up in Elkins Park to sublet with two young women.

"It was like a *Three's Company* kind of deal," Joe remembers, since the show was wildly popular at the time. "People kept making jokes about that. It was kind of a scandal within my own family that I was living in an apartment with two girls. So that tells you something, too, because I wasn't out to them yet."

Though the Philly club scene was awash with queer musicians, zinesters, and promoters, a lack of visibility and a litany of micro-aggressions made none of that evident to Joe. Back home, before he left for Temple, a fishing buddy dispensed the worst advice he's ever received: "Don't be gay." It was meant constructively; Joe would never find true love if he was gay. Nobody would hire him. It was a "choice." Joe took the advice to heart. He decided to remain in the closet, and the AIDS crisis gave him even more reason to avoid addressing it while he found a viable distraction in music.

That fall at 4445 Baker Street was immensely productive. Their earliest recorded version of "I Don't Wanna" put their beloved Ramones into a shambolic blender with *Flex Your Head* and *Let Them Eat Jellybeans!* They were both inspired by hardcore yet had to improvise around not having a drummer. Most of the still-fictional Dead Milkmen songs were built around Dave's bass lines, noticeably "Dance with Me." This arrangement technique would spill over into much of *Big Lizard in My Backyard*, especially "Nutrition," "Swordfish," and one of the best bass intros ever recorded for "Serrated Edge." It would put *Big Lizard* in league with other vaunted post-punk records (e.g., Joy Division's *Unknown Pleasures, Violent Femmes*, and multiple early Cure albums), where the listener could identify almost every song by the bass line.

Concurrently, Rodney started his sophomore year at West Chester State College (soon to become University), concerned about losing his seat at the table. He devoted himself to improving at drums, putting arrangements to all the extant Dead Milkmen songs, and playing along with Vanity 6. He continued mailing Joe lyrics. Some, like "Right

Wing Pigeons" and "Guns for Tots," had been angry screeds influenced by debates in his political science classes. For the year following John Hinckley's attempted assassination of Ronald Reagan in 1981 (and subsequent acquittal on grounds of insanity), the NRA completed its wholesale takeover of the Republican Party, aiming to arm every white American. Morton Grove, Illinois, made national headlines when it passed a law banning all handguns. In a moment of reactionary fervor, Kennesaw, Georgia, passed a law *requiring* every household to own a gun. The town council stuck to a talking point: "If we all have guns, then we won't have crooks." This hyperfixation on gun rights at the expense of all other freedoms would remain a potent thread for the Milkmen. "Violent School" (1985) anticipated the ascendancy of school shootings. They would later position firearms within sacred-cow-slaying revenge fantasies ("Ringo Buys a Rifle"), screeds against toxic masculinity ("If I Had a Gun"), and, in the wake of the 2012 Sandy Hook massacre, a delusional old man's respite from reality ("Welcome to Undertown"). As of this writing, Kennesaw's arcane, impossible-to-enforce gun law is still on the books, and "Right Wing Pigeons"—including an evergreen reference to a "man in the White House who just don't care"—remains in almost every Dead Milkmen set.

Rodney balanced these out with profoundly unserious lyrics to songs like "Spit Sink" and "Taking Retards to the Zoo," both of which Joe and Dave arranged and recorded for *Purgatory Beat*. Joe and Davids' contribution "Shopper Gopper (Gobbler)" remixed Simon and Garfunkel into a tale about a monster who consumed consumers at the mall (perhaps a distant relative of a monster *who only ate hippies*). "Stupid Maryanne," which would become a live staple for the real Dead Milkmen and later resurface on *The Enigma Variations 2* compilation in 1987, originated as a bouncy piano ballad. "Dancing [with Sally] in the Alley" had a droning, repetitive chord progression eerily like the one Joe would append to "Dean's Dream" over Christmas 1983.

By Christmas 1982, when he and Joe recorded "All I Want for Christmas Is a Job" and "Christmas Party" for an unfinished project, David decided to move out. Though he was only twenty-six, sharing a house with three college-age brats was grating. Though he was broke, he wanted his own place, and his brother Joe, still at Temple, was fine with moving into his room. They decided to throw a Christmas party, inviting various buddies from Temple—one of whom was Dave Reckner, who brought Dean Sabatino down from Sellersville. They got wasted and hit it off; David and Joe thought how cool it would be to get a real drummer like him.

David's devotion to character work predated his time in the Milkmen. During slow moments at Von's, he and his brother Joe would call up whatever hapless victim they could find in the phone book. As a prank caller, David was unflappable, committing to a bit for several minutes before starting to veer off the tracks. He developed a cantankerous middle-aged alter ego named (with finesse) Frederick Lettuce (pronounced Leh-TOO-Chay), who would remain a presence for years with the Milkmen.

In 1983, he moved into a monastic one-bedroom apartment on Roosevelt Boulevard in Northeast Philly. Paul Misner, a friend on the third floor, recalls it was just like having a roommate. Cursed with no air-conditioning and little money, he and David would spend their free days riding buses and trains all over the city to stay cool. On occasion, they would call everybody up to Frogger a grill onto a nearby traffic island for an illegal barbecue. Misner remembers the "quality of tenants" in the building plummeting as heroin and crack ravaged Philly. His neighbor across the hall was an infamous gambler named Hank Matthews, who claimed he'd been in jail with G. Gordon Liddy. Hank and David would pile into Paul's tiny apartment, the only one with a TV, to watch football games every weekend.

The courtesy phone in the first-floor hallway became the command center for what Misner and the Schulthise brothers called "the scenario." They would pick a random name in the phone book and develop an elaborate series of misfortunes that had befallen that person. For example, plaster has fallen on the poor guy and his dog, so they called the SPCA. They called a plastic surgeon, and then a roofer, and gave them their randomly chosen victim's number and information. Paul remembers calling their victim, posing as a surgeon to register how exasperated they were at the volume of unsolicited calls. Kurt, having just dropped out of Temple, found an odd solace in these sessions, a magical moment before *69 (get back that line!) and caller ID ruined everything.

Later that year, Rodney Anonymous adopted another alter ego to crank call local radio talk shows. In one instance, "Kens Wadsworth" called in and sang his jingle "I Hate Living in the Suburbs" with his backup singers, the Wadsies (the occupants of 4445 Baker Street). Another crank call where Rodney asked what it was like to touch a corpse, was recorded and later sampled on "Tugena," an experimental demo they recorded in the back room of the basement where he frequently crashed. A similar sicko appeared, through the phone (which Rodney insisted on using during recording, despite how easy a high-pass filter would have been), singing lead on "Nobody Falls Like" on *Not Richard, but Dick*.

When the Dead Milkmen moved in together in "the cave" on West Forty-Fourth Street following their 1985 tour, David took his character work to the next level. Their roommate Andy Chalfen of WXPN, starting the Wishniaks at the time, wrote "his daily crank calls as Fred Lettuce live on in infamy." On January 1, 1986, David adorned his bedroom door with a newspaper headline that juxtaposed "Happy New Year!" with "Ricky Nelson Killed in Air Crash," inspiring the song "Air Crash Museum." As the Dead Milkmen were spending more time on the road, David's near-pathological prank call skills wove his characters into the band's legend.

"Back then, every corporation had a 1-800 number, which was great fun for Dave," Joe Jack told MC Lars on his podcast. "When he got the wanting, [he could] go to a pay phone and just call it. So he got one, let's say it's Hardee's . . . he claimed that there's this thing called a radar burger. He was acting like somebody who was completely out of his mind, but he stayed in character the whole call and whoever on the other end of the phone would say, 'Well, we don't sell the radar burger.'" Dave's anonymous, enraged parent would then berate the fast-food chain for selling a burger with a transmitter in it that kids loved: "So they could know where their friend was who also ate the burger."

Though David had been inducted into the Dead Milkmen universe, he and Joe continued writing songs together apart from Rodney. Their collaborations tended to be less punky and more folky, not fit for an aspiring hardcore band. They'd eventually come up with the name Ornamental Wigwam for their folk-duo jams, one of which was "Watching Scotty Die," a play on "Watching Scotty Grow," an unsettling hit for both Bobby Goldsboro and its writer Mac Davis, that jammed the radio waves in 1970. Songs like "Watching Scotty Grow" and Paul Anka's "(You're) Having My Baby" (a title Joe would ape in 1989 for his Butterfly Fairweather DIY tape *Halvin' My Baby*) constituted an era that Rodney and Joe recall as "peak terrible." Joe and Dave would position their Scotty as a feeble, sickly kid who had been ravaged by corporate polluters (which sounds familiar). David, a lifelong information junkie, obsessively followed a story in the *Inquirer* about Quality Research Labs, a Bensalem company that made *solvents (for home and industry)* and were under indictment for dumping a toxic cocktail down drainpipes and toilets overnight, resulting in ground contamination near the local high school. Having grown up reading about chemical warfare in Vietnam, they invented a solvent called Ortho Orange #42. As much as Joe was still enamored with Bob Dylan and Phil Ochs, the idea of writing a blatant protest song was anathema to Dave.

Ironically, three years later in December 1986, the Dead Milkmen went to Austin to record their third album. Their friends in the band Glass Eye provided a new arsenal, including K. McCarty's warbly violin, and a supportive environment necessary to turn "Watching Scotty Die" into a Dead Milkmen song. To ensure that they wouldn't get sued for libel, they ran the lyrics by their friend Richie Abowitz's father, Milton, who happened to be a lawyer. Milt, rather than remind them this was outside his expertise as a tax attorney, told them they were fine. Joe took his turn singing lead, establishing the practice of him doing one or two songs per record—something that wouldn't create any major problems until later, when the Dead Milkmen agreed to adapt another Ornamental Wigwam song they called their "punk rock nursery rhyme" for the fourth album.

"Watching Scotty Die" would become a favorite deep cut for the Dead Milkmen and the first to blow many fans' minds, especially that of fifteen-year-old Dan Stevens, who was introduced to them via a mixtape in 1993.

"The first song I ever heard was 'Watching Scotty Die,' and I was hooked right away," said Stevens. "When I heard [it], I was like, *This is my band.*"

Years later, in the wake of Dave's death, when he and Stevens were playing together in the Low Budgets, Joe fell into a new chapter as an acoustic solo artist. Whenever somebody invited him to perform, he started playing a mix of old solo songs, Ornamental Wigwam cutouts, and deconstructed Dead Milkmen favorites, especially "Watching Scotty Die." He incorporated a blend of Dylan, Woody Guthrie, and Daniel Johnston tunes, finally giving him his protest-singer moment, with basements, pubs, and community centers full of fans and friends screaming along.

4. "NUTRITION"
THE DEAD MILKMEN VS. HARDCORE

Late in 1980, the Teen Idles gathered in a Washington, DC, living room to cut, fold, and glue the artwork for their band's seven-inch EP *Minor Disturbance*. The rhythm section of the Teen Idles—Ian MacKaye and Jeff Nelson—were starting a new band called Minor Threat and released their former band's EP as Dischord Records No. 1. Today, original pressings sell, conservatively, for well over $500, and this anecdote of DIY legend has been told in multiple coffee-table books.

That same month, in a sunken-level bedroom two hours north in Wagontown, Pennsylvania, Joe Genaro recorded and slightly produced the fifth cassette of lo-fi bedroom guitar pop by "the Dead Milkmen." Half the tracks on *Cows & Gals* featured Garth and Rodney. The handmade artwork featured a cutout of a smiling fifties model laid over a color photo of cows lying behind a barbed-wire fence, like the ones in the pasture across from this house. The songs featured absurd topics like "Bang Bang," about a mad gunman threatening the remaining Beatles (John Lennon had been murdered a week beforehand), and a jumpy number about drug-laced fruits called "Plum(b) Dumb." Within months, his buddy Kurt Brennerman back at Temple would introduce him to the Dead Kennedys. But now, despite his well-worn copy of *Rocket to Russia* sitting nearby, he had no idea a thing called "hardcore punk" existed. Still, this tape was so underground, it was never even *released.*

Despite what a diminishing litany of purists might argue, the Dead Milkmen are a hardcore band. They played with, or were raised on, nearly every canonical band of the American hardcore era. They even canonized *other* bands (some posthumously) simply by name-checking them. They played with JFA, they played with the Minutemen, they played with Flipper, they played with D.O.A., they played with the Circle Jerks, and if Minor Threat hadn't broken up the same month the (real) Dead Milkmen formed, they likely would have played with them too. They deviated so far from the dogma and formula of "hardcore" that they cruised past "post-hardcore" altogether. Still, the Milkmen are every bit as important to Philadelphia as Fugazi is to Washington, DC; both bands have raised incalculable amounts of money and awareness for local causes, both critiqued jockish moshers and crowd-surfers (in slightly different manners), both were produced by Ted Niceley, both had drummers inspired/trained by jazz greats, both have ruthlessly quotable front men, and both have performed "Waiting Room" in Washington, DC. However, Fugazi were "black coffee," and the Milkmen are *a cool Coors 16-ouncer*, served with filet of sole.

"When we started, we used to play a lot of the hardcore scene," Dean told *Central Michigan Life* in October 1986, "but that was because it was the available medium to do the music we wanted to play. But our music style is really hard to put into words because it varies so much from song to song. We'll play a country song and then a funk song and maybe some harder stuff, but when it comes right down to it, it's all just rock 'n' roll."

"I would compare [the Dead Milkmen] to an East Coast version of Phoenix's own Sun City Girls," said Sean Bonnette, founder of AJJ, an Arizona folk-punk band who cite *Beelzebubba* as a "DNA-level" influence. "They're both really prolific, long-running bands that don't really give a shit about the 'form' of punk and are happy to play in a bunch of different genres just because they can and it's fun, while at the same time like throwing around extremely gnarly ideas and topics and taking the piss out of anyone that would take themselves too seriously."

The Milkmen and Girls played together twice—once in July 1984 with JFA at a UPenn frat party, and once at the Masquerade in Atlanta in November 1992. At the latter gig, the large crowd who had assembled for the (rescheduled) Milkmen date *hated* Sun City Girls. One drunken fan even invaded the stage to interrupt their set. Bassist Alan Bishop threw the guy off the stage in one smooth motion, and they kept playing while the Milkmen laughed their asses off. Later, Rodney admonished the crowd, yelling "Sun City Girls walk on water in their spare time!"

The Dead Milkmen were well used to feeding off crowd anger.

"Nutrition," the closing track on *Big Lizard in My Backyard,* was a roundabout tribute to the Philly hardcore scene that Joe demoed for his bandmates in early 1984. The lyrics come from a character like the teenage burnout of "V.F.W." who uses his parents' credit card with abandon like the "Bitchin' Camaro" driver. It lionizes and satirizes the hardcore scene—the narrator gets increasingly juvenile, ending the song with a line about his mom making him clean his plate if he wants to go see Flag of Democracy. At one point, our narrator declares that they'll "just hang out on Broad and South, living by [their] intuition." That intersection was, for several pivotal years, the home to Love Hall. Between June 1982 and February 1984, local wrestling luminary Howard Saunders booked at least twenty shows, including the Misfits, Necros, Crucifucks, Negative Approach, T.S.O.L., Jodie Foster's Army (JFA), and Minor Threat. On July 2, 1983, a fire in a flophouse hotel next door threatened to (and probably should have) shut the venue down, but it kept going.

"I have very distinct memories of being in homeroom, and people being like, 'What did you do this weekend?'" recalls Electric Love Muffin bassist Brian Campbell. "'Oh, I went to see this band Hüsker Dü with the Minutemen in this burned-out [place] called Love Hall.' When you would come out, your snot would be completely black."

On Friday, June 10, 1983, Minor Threat brought out a fanatical crew, including all three Schulthise brothers, Paul Misner, Joe Genaro, and Chuck Meehan, whose band YDI played just about every hardcore hovel in the city. Minor Threat had been unraveling—this would be one of their final gigs—but the show, which included local support from McRad and Autistic Behavior, left lifelong impacts. For one, Kurt Schulthise is convinced that the throbbing pile of screaming humans fucked up his oldest brother's back, leaving David with spinal pain for the rest of his life. Second, David and Joe had a fire lit under them to find a solid drummer and book a damn show.

"It was actually the first time [Minor Threat] played in Philadelphia proper," said Meehan. "And it was kind of funny that they played all around the country before they got to play even Philadelphia."

Other than rough luck for Meehan and his cohort, there were reasons for this. On July 10, 1981, Black Flag were booked to play the Starlite Ballroom, a decrepit theater in Kensington, a tough-as-nails neighborhood northeast of downtown. The venue was familiar with punk and hardcore, hosting the Circle Jerks one month prior, but on the night of Black Flag everything that could have gone wrong did. Opening the show were harDCore kids S.O.A., whose singer, Henry Garfield, was preparing to move to LA and become Black Flag singer Henry Rollins. Philly locals Autistic Behavior rounded out the bill.

"That show should have been Philadelphia hardcore's coming-out party!" Meehan said. Instead, it turned into an all-out war between the DC day-trippers and Kensington locals. The following November, Minor Threat played an infamous gig at Buff Hall across the river in Camden with Boston's SS Decontrol and New York's Agnostic Front. Two decades after the Sabatino family left, Camden had fallen noticeably deeper into decay. After-hours, it was largely the province of Black biker gangs with whom the hardcore kids had made peace. Before Minor Threat loaded in, a psychotic motorist plowed into their tour van, sending Ian MacKaye to the hospital. He got stitched up in time to play the gig, though.

Such false starts repeatedly hobbled Philly's hardcore scene. In 1983, WXPN DJ Eddie Hacksaw, not to be outdone by DC's *Flex Your Head* (Dischord, 1982) or Boston's *This Is Boston, Not L.A.* (Modern Method 1982), scrambled to release *Get Off My Back: We're Doing It Ourselves*. Unfortunately, its crude recordings undercut the participating bands. Philadelphia proto-punk bands like the all-Black Pure Hell, who could have cleaned the stage with the New York Dolls, "went unheard for like twenty-five years until the internet came out," said Chuck Meehan. Bands like Ruin, YDI, and Flag of Democracy were footnotes when American hardcore started to receive the coffee-table treatment. Professionally published and distributed books started appearing as hardcore turned twenty(ish). One of the first, and best, was *Dance of Days*, a DC-focused 2001 collaboration by Mark Andersen and Mark Jenkins (the latter of whom had panned *Beelzebubba* in the *Washington Post* in 1988). Shortly thereafter, Steven Blush's *American Hardcore* zoomed out and presented a nationwide "tribal history." Blush *hated* the Dead Milkmen—a fact they still laugh off. It wasn't until 2007 that George Hurchalla gave the Philly scene and the Dead Milkmen props in his book *Going Underground: American Punk 1979–1989*. In it, he explained why the Milkmen, however unintentionally, rose above their counterparts: "If you were a Philly punk who got to see the bands live in their prime, you knew a lot of them were pretty great. But to outsiders, it sure didn't look like much worthwhile was going on."

Hacksaw's compilation—the only official release for most of the bands included—was also difficult to find; Rodney Linderman and Joe Genaro both discovered hardcore via LPs exported from California. For Rodney, it was *Hell Comes to Your House*, a 1981 compilation by Jimmy Bemis of the Long Beach band Modern Warfare (whose guitarist, Ron Goudie, would later work for Enigma and produce Mojo Nixon records). Blessed with national distribution, the LP made its way to a record shop in West Chester. The terrifying cover of *Hell* sold him quickly, and Rodney became a fast fan of gothy groups like Christian Death, 45 Grave, 100 Flowers (formerly the Urinals), and a pre-heroin, pre-greaser Social Distortion. The following year, Better Youth Organization (BYO) issued the *Someone Got Their Head Kicked In!* compilation, which turned Rodney on to the Adolescents and Battalion of Saints.

"The year that *Thriller* came out, I spent my money on *Mommy's Little Monster*, and I'm still proud of that fact!" he loudly declared onstage in Baltimore in 2009, days after Michael Jackson's death.

"Milkman Story" Take on Raymond Pettibon's artwork for Black Flag's "Police Story." Sketch from a 1983 Rodney Linderman letter to Joe Genaro. Courtesy of Joe Genaro.

In early 1981, Joe's friend Kurt Brennerman rewired his brain with a tape that included a couple of especially speedy songs by Dead Kennedys. It was the fastest thing he'd ever heard, and whenever he could get together with Rodney and Garth back home, they started speeding up their recordings. Joe's affinity for hardcore was somewhat unique; rather than the often-cited anger and aggression, the bouncy BPM of D. H. Peligro and Jeff Nelson reminded him of joyful, festive music like polka. Once he started playing an electric guitar, he was also less committed to generating a wall of distortion like East Bay Ray or Lyle Preslar.

"I didn't have any distortion pedals—or any pedals [at all] for that matter back then," he told *Guitar World.* "I tried out a borrowed pedal once in practice, but it wasn't working with the band. My sound was just my Gibson SG plugged into a Yamaha G100-112. Any distortion came from the amp itself. It was considered a rather clean sound compared to other punk bands."

This made Joe, like D. Boon, seem innovative and brave to the next few generations of punk nerds. One of many was the Sword's guitarist Kyle Shutt, who moved to Austin, Texas, in an Elsie shirt from dusty Odessa around the turn of the millennium.

"Growing up in the Philly punk scene, [Joe] was singled out a lot, and I think he learned not to make a target out of himself," said Shutt, "[but] he's very brave. It takes a lot of fuckin' balls to play with absolutely no overdrive whatsoever. I think that's way braver than hiding behind a wall of amps."

As loud, fast, and aggressive as Philly's answers to Bad Brains were, there is little question that, in terms of bending the young Milkmen's mind, no local band could touch the Stick Men. Joe had never seen anything like them, eagerly reporting back to Rodney that they were "like James Brown, but with a lot more energy." The duo made it a point to see them at the East Side Club that July, and Rodney fell in love with their catatonic skronks. Though there exists a common misconception that "No Wave" was tethered to New York's Lower East Side in 1978, Peter L. Baker and B.A.L. (Beth Ann Lejman) Stack could have kicked Arto Lindsay and Lydia Lunchs' asses up and down Avenue A. The Stick Men were a "punk rock Sun Ra," as Dave Reckner reminisced. He and Dean, still reticent about risking life and limb in dank Philly neighborhoods, took advantage of the band's gallery shows in Allentown.

As the real Milkmen gradually took form going into 1983, "being like the Stick Men" was a unifying goal. Today, it's impossible to un-hear that influence on the *Big Lizard* cut "Lucky," which anxiously speeds up. Nearly thirty years later, Rodney penned another nod to the Stick Men called "Ronald Reagan Killed the Black Dahlia" (Joe: "Say *what?*") for their 2013 singles series. Tragically, a blend of personal issues and a very Lower-East-Side-like taste for narcotics unraveled the Stick Men (Peter Baker passed in 1994) long before they could enjoy any posthumous attention. Rodney still contends they're the greatest band to ever come from Philadelphia.

The first place Joe saw the Stick Men was the Elks Lodge at Sixteenth and Fitzwater. By 1981, it was the closest thing Philly had to an all-ages venue for fast-and-loud bands. A local group who called themselves the Swingerz booked UK goth progenitors Bauhaus in 1980, and it took off from there, at least for a little while.

"I later learned [the Elks Lodge] was an unbelievably historic place," said Nancy Barile, author of *I'm Not Holding Your Coat*, which includes the first granular look at the Philly scene. "It should never have been torn down. They even had Bessie Smith's funeral there. . . . The Black Elks started their own Elks, and they were really good to us. We could rent from them for maybe $200, we had to get a PA. Sound wasn't super good, but it was a fun place to do shows . . . until somebody broke the bathrooms and then they didn't want to rent to us anymore."

On Saturday, October 3, 1981, Barile booked a show for the Sadistic Exploits, Informed Sources, Autistic Behavior, and Decontrol. The audience included Joe Genaro, then in his second year at Temple, attending his first full-on hardcore show. Within weeks of that Elks show, Joe and his roommate Dan Mapp would venture out to a basement show at Dave Reckner's house to see a Devo-adjacent duo he "managed" called Narthex. Having spent a year trying to find gigs for his Bucks County friends, he threw up his hands and had them play at his house. Genaro was too shy to do anything other than marvel at this seedy underworld he'd stumbled into. It helped stoke the fire that would manifest in the *Living Death in the Cellar of Sin* tape that Joe, Rodney, and Garth made that Thanksgiving break in Wagontown. That winter break, Joe and Rodney would collaborate on *Nine New Sins by the Dead Milkmen*, putting to tape the earliest versions of "Stupid Mary Anne," "Don't Abort That Baby," and "Dance with Me," two of which they would rerecord for *A Date with the Dead Milkmen*.

For all his misgivings on the Milkmen, Steven Blush did admit that by the mid-eighties, most of the people he knew in the Philly scene were too fucked up to be paying attention.

"We probably got more attention nationally than the others, but at the same time, we were not totally embraced as a hardcore band," said Genaro. "We didn't really play what a lot of people thought a hardcore band was, but neither did

McRad or F.O.D. really."

Bands like Soul Glo, who, like the Milkmen, are impossible to imagine coming from anywhere but Philly, have helped elevate Philadelphia in the conversation about how hardcore needed to consistently reinvent itself to stay so relevant. And most remarkably, anyone around the city, to this day, can still *go to the hardcore show and see F.O.D.*

5. "BITCHIN' CAMARO"
THE DEAD MILKMEN VS. THE ROAD

The story of "Bitchin' Camaro," the inimitable piece of punk rock Vaudeville that *put* the Dead Milkmen on the road, is the story of five car accidents (and one harrowing near-accident). Ironically, the Dead Milkmen are largely either nondrivers or poor drivers. Car wrecks showed all over in their early lyrics (e.g., Little Billy hitting a tree and exploding on impact in "Lucky"), and they occasionally weaved wrecks into their origin story. In the zine *Still Thinking* in 1987, they claimed Joe and Rodney collided with Dave and Dean after going the wrong way on a cloverleaf exit, asking Dean if he wanted to be in a band when they saw his drum kit.

"That's how I wrecked his car," said Joe, likely flashing a Harpo-like smile.

Crash One: Upper Bucks County, 1978
Shortly after getting his license, the lanky, six-foot-tall, popular tri-sport athlete David Reckner broke his leg in three places in a traumatic wreck near his home in Ambler. After six weeks in the hospital, he couldn't even jog without his knee swelling up. His old friendships at Pennridge High

School, largely predetermined by team sports, withered, and he fell into a deep depression.

"When I came out of it, Steve Wallis and Dean were really the only two people that [were there for me]," Reckner said. "I was kind of like this ghost to the rest of the population."

Reckner poured himself into the UHF production department, helping Dean and Steve produce *Sab & Wally*, along with numerous other local shows. The "creative stuff" gave him a community again, and he turned his attention to becoming a sound guy. Upon graduation in 1980, he courted an offer with a local UHF station, which his well-off parents urged him to turn down in favor of a college career at Temple. In his freshman year at Temple's Radio-TV-Film program, he made the acquaintance of classmates Dan Mapp and Joe Genaro. Dean Sabatino, also a scrawny suburbanite who had time to burn after his Art Institute classes ended for the day, would come over to Temple and find his buddy Dave, frequently sitting in on his classes, where he made the acquaintance of Joe.

Reckner also found a gig doing sound at Comedy Works, where he befriended a novice comic named Chris Coccia, who quickly connected with Dean over a shared passion for art and photography. Had Reckner not endured the traumatic accident, the history of the Dead Milkmen could have been drastically different. Either way, the photo on the cover wouldn't be as cool.

Crash Two: Somewhere Between Caln and Wagontown, Pennsylvania

On a fateful stop at Wawa in 1983, prodigal eavesdropper Rodney stood in line behind two "dudes" excited to go "down the shore." They tossed the term "bitchin'" around to the point where Rodney nearly cracked.

"In the eighties, we called each other 'dude' sarcastically because it was making fun of frat bros," says Andy Chalfen, who became a major "Bitchin'" proponent at WXPN. "The 'bro' culture, which was toxic then, now it's just infected everything. It was just so refreshing, [with] the Milkmen, life didn't have to be that way."

Arguably inspired by Adrenalin O.D.'s "Trans Am" (according to George Hurchalla) and unquestionably motivated after the band's first gig, Rodney presented Joe with a set of lyrics written from the point of view of one of these spoiled brats. Joe quickly put a chord progression to it, and by early August all four of the Dead Milkmen were in the same room and practicing together. Joe and Rodney improvised a two-minute Vaudevillian vamp of a conversation over David's walking bass line and Dean's cocktail-lounge fills. The earliest known recording (with background laughter) was captured in the Sabatino basement for *Millersville Delivery*, a tape the Dead Milkmen recorded for a friend to play at the eponymous university.

That January, when Joe was at home for winter break, Rod was on his way over to Wagontown. He lost control and drove onto a highway median outside Coatesville, winding up upside down. It was a miracle that he crawled out of it. His father fixed the car and agreed to keep it at their house, but Rodney refused to get behind the wheel again. As the band's local following accrued—necessitating weekly practice time—Linderman was the only one of the Milkmen who had wheels. David's '68 Impala (alias "ghetto cruiser") barely survived the trip back from Indiana in 1981. Dean's Volkswagen Beetle had long been falling apart— likely why Reckner had to provide wheels for his "audition" in Manayunk—and he had the most accessible basement and most tolerant parents. He and his kit weren't moving.

"Rodney wouldn't drive [his car] because of that accident, but he let me drive it," recalls Genaro. "So, I would take a bus from Philly, while I was going to Temple, into West Chester. And then either Rodney's dad or my dad would pick me up at the bus station and drive me to Rodney's house. And then I would get in Rodney's car and drive to West Chester University and pick Rodney up. Then I would drive to where Dave was living, pick him up, and then drive Rodney's car to Dean's house, where we practiced."

Then he would do it all in reverse, spending Sunday night in Wagontown before his dad drove him back to the Philly bus before work on Monday morning.

"We would do it weekend after weekend like that," Joe says. "It seems insane to me now, but that's how we got the band to go to practices. The energy you have when you're a kid."

That spring, WCU's 1984 Air Band competition became the straw that ended Rodney's undergraduate career. He and his girlfriend Barbara (known to friends as B.J.) decided to enter the competition with a favorite *Let Them Eat Jellybeans* track: "Jesus Entering from the Rear" by the Feederz. The committee rejected their submission and gave Rodney and Barbara an hour to pick an alternative. A year prior, townie sophomore Rodney Linderman may not have chosen violence. But now, they were dealing with Rodney Anonymous of the Dead Milkmen.

"We wanted to make the students aware of this injustice! This time it was us, the next time it could be you!" Rod and B.J. wrote in an editorial in *The Quad* newspaper on March 27, cosigned by 315 members of the West Chester student community. The university, along with the student radio station WCUR, responded by equating atheism with hate speech, opining for some reason that "minorities keep wanting more and more." Barbara's mother, Jean M. Robb, a self-professed "right-winged conservative" and longtime mayor of Deerfield Beach, Florida, wrote a letter apologizing for her daughter's "misguided zeal." Rodney's mother, on the other hand, was pissed off at WCU, and started showing up to Dead Milkmen gigs as soon as she could. She nearly got rejected from the Chestnut Cabaret for stage diving before the security were informed who she was. She remained a fan for the rest of her life. Jean M. Robb wound up leaving office following ethics violations.

Whether or not Rodney survived his final semester at WCU, it ended in a small triumph as a fast-tightening Dead Milkmen took to the airwaves at WXPN on Sunday, May 6, 1984. They recorded seventeen songs in a half hour, including an amended "Veterans of a Censored World" that would quickly circulate on cassette as *The Dead Milkmen Take the Airwaves*. Philadelphia was in love.

Crash Three: Mötley Crüe's Lead Singer

By the end of 1984, Mötley Crüe were conquering MTV and rock radio with two best-selling albums. The first, 1981's *Too Fast for Love*, was the breakout release for Enigma Records—a gambit that cofounder Wesley Hein is still shocked paid off for him and his brother Bill. Enigma stayed in the Sunset Strip game for years, releasing albums for Christian hair band Stryper, as well as Pennsylvania transplants Poison (whose record *Look What the Cat Dragged In* could be seen getting mangled in the 1989 video for "Punk Rock Girl" by labelmates the Dead Milkmen).

On December 8, Crüe singer Vince Neil took his buddy Nicholas Dingley (alias Razzle) for a drunken ride in his De Tomaso Pantera with the purpose of getting drunker. Razzle was the British drummer for the Finnish band Hanoi Rocks, a rare firebomb of glam-metal beloved as much by critics as by fans. Neil swerved to avoid a fire truck while going 65 mph in a 25 mph zone, colliding with two other motorists, killing Razzle on impact.

Less than two weeks later, on December 20, the Dead Milkmen met at Third Story Recording to lay down ten tracks for an EP with "Bitchin' Camaro" as the centerpiece. In the take used on *Big Lizard in My Backyard*, Joe announces his intentions to "play some video games [and] buy some Def Leppard T-shirts" at the shore, and Rodney reminds him to buy Mötley Crüe T-shirts, because "all proceeds go to get their lead singer out of jail." On an alternate take, which the band unveiled in 2025, Joe said Def Leppard and Mötley Crüe T-shirts, and Rodney replies about "what an unsafe driver their lead singer is!" Fortunately, the line about getting Vince Neil out of jail was funnier and more evergreen.

By early 1985, around when *another* car accident would derail and then rerail the Milkmen's career, Hanoi Rocks decided to fold. Mötley Crüe, concurrently, shifted to glam rock to roaring success. Vince Neil spent barely any time in jail.

Crash Four: Somewhere Between Wisconsin and Illinois
Going into those December sessions, the Milkmen planned to self-release a 45 rpm EP like their SST heroes Hüsker Dü and Meat Puppets. Dan Mapp, who was living well as a regional rep for RCH Cable, had arranged to finance the

pressing. In 1983, he and David Herzog, another Temple RTF major, played as the Singles, including a gig opening for the Dead Milkmen on July 23 at the Harleysville Youth Center. His job soon moved Dan to the breathtaking Lake Superior college town of Marquette, Michigan, followed by a letdown in the rural sundown town of Granite City, Illinois. Whenever he had an excuse, he would drive up to Chicago for shows, especially whenever his old friends came out from Philly.

One night in early 1985, he and a companion were driving along a rural road. It was late, cold, and wet out, with annoyingly limited visibility. Out of nowhere, as Mapp recalls the split-second motion, he saw two dogs walk into the road. He swerved to avoid them, lost traction, and the next thing he remembers was his car skidding to a halt on its side. He and his passenger were both fine, which was more than could be said for his wallet.

"We were picking songs for the record," Mapp recalls, "and it actually worked out better for them that that happened, because then they had to go through regular channels."

Unfortunately, Philly lacked most regular channels. Their fans were, by and large, broke, and nobody rich would pour money into a hardcore band with no touring experience. Packing out frat parties every other weekend at Pi Lam did not get attention from anyone in New York. Los Angeles and Nashville may as well have been on other planets.

Fortunately, a UPenn professor ran a label that was far from regular. Colin Camerer had been a child prodigy who, after entering Johns Hopkins University at age fourteen, completed his PhD in economics at the University of

Chicago in 1981. Concurrently with his PhD work, he and a friend started a record label as an experiment. Camerer had noticed something awry about record sales reporting as the disco era was deflating.

"*Billboard*, which was the main source of information, didn't actually use record sales," he said of the pre-barcode era. "Our conviction at the time was that punk music had a bigger market than was being reported and it was not a bad investment on kind of a shoestring. . . . I remember hearing R.E.M. [on WNUR at Northwestern] when they were first coming out. The college radio stations were really clued in. I mean, part of it was, that was their niche. When bands got too famous, it became uninteresting."

His first signees for Fever Records were local punks the Effigies, regulars at the Cubby Bear who figured prominently on Chicago's first wider punk releases. One such release, *The Middle of America*, was compiled by Northwestern undergrad Doug Conn on his label Hope Is Dangerous (H.I.D.). Conn had started WNUR's first punk show, "Fast and Loud," which ran for years after he graduated and moved to Philly in 1984 for his master's in communications. It didn't feel like Philadelphia had the deepest bench of punk or hardcore bands, despite its primal location in the Megalopolis. The one band he kept on coming back to, though, was the Dead Milkmen.

"Joe wrote songs in [all these] different styles, and I remember his ballads used to get the attention of the girls in the audience," Conn said. "Rodney's talk-sing style was unique. It made me think of Suicidal Tendencies, and then the Offspring later. Not many bands could pull it off."

The year prior, the Baltimore native Camerer had relocated to Philly for a job teaching at the Wharton School of Business at UPenn, taking half of Fever Records with him to his new apartment on Fourth Street. WXPN quickly united Colin and Doug's disparate paths, largely under the aegis of music director Mike Morrison. At the time, Morrison sang and played guitar in the Johnsons, one of Philly's entries into the jangle-pop underground. Camerer agreed to release an album by the Milkmen so long as they went back to Third Story and recorded enough tracks to stretch it to a full-length LP. He also wanted them to go out to Chicago and play the Cubby Bear to prove they were "road ready." They obliged, returning to the studio on February 13, 1985. Joe was severely ill with a head cold, but he persevered by chugging cough syrup between takes before succumbing to dehydration. On the cut of "Rastabilly" that made it onto *Big Lizard*, Rodney pokes fun at Joe being "all messed up on cough syrup, so . . . nevermind."

With their Cubby Bear gig booked for later that month, Camerer made good on his agreement, signing the Dead Milkmen to Fever Records on March 7, 1985. Per his clause, Jerrock Tapes ceased operations, making the hand-duped cassettes like *Funky Farm* and *Someone Shot Sunshine* into true relics of their early mailing list. Despite having no manager, a hands-off financier for a label, and no van, Dave Blood took matters into his own hands and dug into *Maximumrocknroll*. He called and mailed a bunch of promoters and venues, got feedback on a string of dates, and possibly owing to the potentially hefty long-distance bill, didn't bother to confirm any of them.

Locally, the Milkmen booked an assortment of gigs with the Johnsons and Fabulous Fondas to stay fresh and work on new material. Days after shipping their master tapes out for pressing, they scored a hot weekend of shows. The first was Friday night, May 4 with Redd Kross and White Flag at the C.E. Center, where most hardcore-inclusive shows had migrated after Love Hall gave up the ghost. The second was on Saturday at the Kennel Club, "headlining" a convention for the Church of the SubGenius, a Dallas-based organization the *Inquirer* called the "weirdest supercult." The Kennel Club's booker, David Wildmann, welcomed the off-center programming. Rodney Anonymous thought this was the coolest. These weirdos were their people. His bandmates went along with it; they would never say no to Wildmann.

Joe, Dean, and Rodney performing for the Church of the SubGenius convention at the Kennel Club, May 5, 1985. Photo by Chris Coccia.

As the weekend approached, David's sinusitis flared back up, and he needed emergency surgery. Having confirmed with the SubGenius and having been featured in their unhinged advertising, the band asked Mike Morrison to fill in on bass. Having seen the band dozens of times and having all their tapes at WXPN, Morrison could handle the task. The other three Milkmen felt between a rock and a hard place, and would never dream of replacing him permanently, but Dave Blood was pissed. The incident put David even more on his heels. As he approached thirty, he got increasingly stealthy at downplaying physical and mental issues at the risk of being a liability.

(Nearly) Crash: Deep in the Heart of Texas

In June, the band geared up for two months on the road that would net them roughly fifty dollars per night in a six-week stretch that Dean remembers as "pretty much a disaster." Rodney's father loaned them their family's conversion van with the expectation that it would return without, say, nearly losing a wheel in rural Texas or getting fucked up by an Oklahoma car wash. The band convinced adult-in-the-room Reckner to join as their sound guy. They also needed help with driving, since Rodney still refused to, and David couldn't with his eye problem. Reckner thought, *Why not—* at least he wouldn't have to do any booking, right?

"I started doing very 'managerial' things [after] we'd show up at places that weren't expecting us," said Reckner. "Then I wound up calling the label on a regular basis and trying to get them to do things for us, which wasn't very fruitful."

The tour's routing, which Reckner describes as "looney tunes," would bring the Milkmen out to Los Angeles, where Enigma Records (and their indie wing, Reckless), who had signed a pressing and distribution deal with Fever, had provided $1,800 in credit to support the band on the road. The band's bad luck started over a week before they even *hit* the road. They booked a *Big Lizard in My Backyard* record-release party with the Fabulous Fondas for Thursday, June 20, at Bacchanal, an "artsy gutter-drunk" bar in a rough neighborhood at Thirteenth and South. A distribution snafu by Enigma delayed their LPs shipping to Philly until the following weekend, when they kicked off their "tour" over in Atlantic City, opening for D.O.A. and the Dicks at the Elks Lodge. Armed with a variety of tapes of their Philly phriends like the Johnsons, Psychotic Norman, and the Electric Love Muffin, they headed out West.

"We used that [1985] demo tape extensively . . . the Milkmen were always super supportive as far as being advocates, not only for us, but for a lot of bands in Philadelphia," said Love Muffin bassist Brian Campbell. "It's something they still do today. It's an inherent part of their DNA."

The actual tour started with "Thrashorama '85" on June 30, at a Pittsburgh nightclub called the Electric Banana, whose owner Johnny had a reputation that preceded him. After the gig, it was time to get the hundred bucks they were owed—and an alleged bonus for selling one hundred tickets on a Sunday night. The band nominated Reckner for the simple reason that he was the tallest. Assuming a "managerial" expression, he walked up to the office and knocked on the door. After a moment of terse negotiations, Johnny here's-your-fuckin'-money'd him the cash. Reckner took a breath and brought up the bonus. Johnny Banana showed him a revolver. Reckner power-walked away, the band gathered their equipment, and they got the hell out of there. It wouldn't be the last time Reckner had a gun pulled on him that summer.

They played a promising gig at Stache's in Columbus the following night en route to Chicago for one of their anchor gigs at the Cabaret Metro with the Circle Jerks. A friendly stagehand informed Joe that it may be prudent to, on occasion, wipe down his strings—a new piece of knowledge for him. A stop at the Wax Trax! record store in Chicago included one of the first indications that *Big Lizard* was out in the world. Dean wouldn't see his cover art in print until reading *The Gavin Report* (a contemporary to *College Music Journal*) in Los Angeles, but the shop had the LP prominently displayed.

After an optimistic night at the Cabaret Metro, where the venue's workers carried the band's equipment (an incomparable luxury for the Milkmen at the time), they drove down to West Lafayette to celebrate the Fourth with David's buddy Stewart, who lived in and managed a trailer park adjacent to Purdue's campus. Since 1978, he had lived there in a pink eight-by-forty, soon becoming the lot manager to save the twenty-five dollars in monthly rent.

"I guess it's a freedom of sorts, but the thing is, chicks don't love it when they find out you live in a fuckin' trailer," Frescas laughs. "Architecture students would always be coming out there taking pictures, because it was the epitome of the trashy trailer park."

In the prime of his young professional years in West Lafayette, Stewart had a three-pronged reputation. To members of the Purdue community, he was a jolly beardo riding around town on vintage bicycles. To a smattering of local punks and burnouts, he was a righteous rocker known for the ragers in his park. If you asked his employers at Great Lakes Chemical, he was a radical piss-ant agitator. All three were correct.

"The music scene in this town has always been kind of on life support," he said, "so that, like, this was like a breath of fresh air and people didn't give a damn that it was punk music. It was something new."

That Fourth of July would be the first meeting between Stewart and the rest of the Dead Milkmen. What he lacked in technical know-how—bringing in a tinny PA hardly suitable for a rock band—he made up for in enthusiasm.

"They were a little green behind the gills themselves, as far as being the touring band," said Frescas. "I got a PA and then their stage was a bunch of pallets that were stacked up. It was on the Fourth of July, [and] I don't know where I got this flag for the Soviet Union, but it was flying above the trailer park. They were playing and all these people came."

The following year, Stewart would sign an affidavit charging that his employer had mishandled hazardous materials, setting off an illegal retaliation by Great Lakes Chemical that would chase him from Indiana until things cooled down. He would hide out in Philadelphia with the Milkmen, even going on the road with them—his unique set of skills made him an effective security guy and roadie. "Stuart," one of the Milkmen's greatest "hits," was a roundabout tribute to his whistleblowing and his trailer park (though they changed the spelling to both protect the innocent and nod to Austin recording engineer Stuart Sullivan).

The remainder of July 1985 was a blur of unconfirmed dates, sweltering heat, slingshotting back and forth to Sheila Sullivan's place in Chicago, Reckner phone calls, the dusty open road, and Dean nearly strangling Rodney with his bare hands. In Minneapolis one week after Stewart's barbecue, their gig at Seventh Street Entry was pleasant, though the band they played before, Ring Theatre, was a slog. While Dean and Rodney were covering the dressing room drywall with profane messages, they heard a commotion: Prince and Sheila E. had shown up and played a three-minute jam on

Ring Theatre's bass and drums. Twin Cities regulars were accustomed to this, but to the Dead Milkmen, it was one of the most surreal experiences of their lives. Rodney had pushed himself to learn drums along with Vanity 6 records, and now he was locked in a tiny club with their mentor, one of the biggest stars on the planet. Right after finishing, Prince, Sheila E., and their wall of bodyguards vanished into the night.

At their next stop, Madison, they played some of their best sets of the whole tour (perhaps empowered by the Purple one) and then wreaked belligerent havoc on a frat party—*a bad party, the worst party that's ever been*—at the University of Wisconsin. The Milkmen, Reckner, and two girls from their show got the house of "rude and strange people" practically condemned. They spilled beer everywhere, and at one point, Reckner, Joe, and Rodney all unloaded their bladders into the fireplace. Thanks to a party trick Rodney recalled from his life at a "cow college," they convinced the girl collecting money at the door to refund them—twice—before they actually left around 4 a.m.

Once they left the tether of the Midwest and headed South, things got even messier. The gig Dave Blood had "booked" in Denver fell through, and they kept their fingers crossed that things would pick up in Oklahoma. They didn't. The band played to a crowd of thirty in Norman for seventy-four dollars, and their gig the following night in Tulsa was canceled. The next day, Reckner suggested they take the van for a free car wash with fill-up, and it got jammed in the car wash's guide rail. Rodney nearly had a nervous breakdown and things almost escalated to an international incident. Reckner even made up a story that his brother was a big-time lawyer in Philly before one of the workers was, miraculously, able to disengage the guide rail from the van. They had a gracious host, Michelle, whose boyfriend Wayne called the house every five minutes to ensure these Cheesesteaks weren't getting fresh with her. Despite his rabid jealousy, Wayne and Michelle stayed together as common-law partners until 2012, during which time Wayne's band, the Flaming Lips, became alternative rock stars.

The next day, the band's luck somehow got both worse and miraculously better. The Dead Milkmen could easily have been their generation's Exploding Hearts—leaving one undeniable record behind and generations of punk fans wondering *what could have been*. Or, more blatantly, as Dave Blood dryly commented in the zine *Ink Disease*, they would have been the literally Dead Milkmen. With Dean at the wheel somewhere outside Amarillo, the van started shaking violently. They pulled over and hopped out. The tires looked fine. Joe arched his eyebrow and went to check the right rear tire, which he and Reckner had changed back in Kansas City. He lunged for the lug nut . . . and it popped into his palm before he could touch it. The pins had all sheared, the tire held on by a thread.

They managed to flag down a "real Texas stereotype" of a farmer to drive Dean into town to get a wrecker. They got the van towed to Amarillo, where the band checked into a Motel 6, and Reckner got on the phone with Ron Goudie at Enigma. In 1982, his band had released *Hell Comes to Your House*, the compilation that got Rodney and thousands of other kids into hardcore. Now, he was the poor sap assigned to this "Dead Milkmen" account. Reckner remembers that conversation as clear as day.

He admitted to Goudie that he and the band had been plowing through their label credit. Ron asked him how they'd even gotten that far in the first place.

"Well," Dave replied jokingly, "I guess we've got benevolent parents."

"What does that mean?" asked Goudie.

"Oh, well, we were able to borrow a van from Rodney's dad and . . ."

"No, no, no, back it up! What does that word mean: *benevolent?*"

Reckner was speechless. This did not portend well for their arrival in LA a few days later. Goudie and Jan Ballard had been asked to book some shows for them around Los Angeles but hadn't. At least the Milkmen had a pleasant base of operations with Reckner's aunt out in "old Irvine," earning the Orange County city a mention in "The Thing That Only Eats Hippies." Still, by this point, they were one month into the tour, with twelve shows under their belts. Looney tunes.

Despite hearing that *Big Lizard* was doing well on the college charts (midsummer was an understandably slow time for college radio), they got a frosty reception at Enigma. They were told to sit down and quietly wait in the office, which highly irked Dean. Though Dave Blood couldn't eat it, Enigma got them Hawaiian pizzas—a novelty that hadn't made it to the East Coast yet. After sitting around, the band became restless and started milling about. Suddenly, Bill Hein cornered Rodney and told them they all had to leave, because some of the staff were convinced the Milkmen were "stealing records."

After playing swiftly booked and horribly promoted gigs—one of which was to an audience of one very nice couple—Reckner, David, and Joe returned to Enigma three days later to a king's reception. What the hell had happened?

They discovered that word got back that "Bitchin' Camaro" had debuted at No. 19 on the college charts. It was nice to feel respected for the first time on the road, but it also validated their collective skepticism of the "industry." Ironically, four years later, the Electric Love Muffin *did* steal six boxes of their second LP *Rassafranna* while on a tour of the Restless/Enigma warehouse; they were frustrated that the label poured resources into the thirteen-year-old punk duo Old Skull and their novelty single "Hot Dog Hell," which came out the same week. Philly bands got *no respect*.

As their tour-diary song "Six Days" would allude on *Eat Your Paisley!*, their stop in Austin (almost) balanced out all the trials of the tour. Their friends in Glass Eye, whom they'd met the previous summer in Philly, were a sight for sore eyes.

"I asked Rodney how much was the most money they'd made, and he said somebody gave them $150," Brian Beattie remembers. "So we gave him $200 just so they would say the very most money they made would have been with us."

Their show in town was a casual affair, with the bands making flyers at Kinko's and walking around town putting them up the day beforehand. Generous crowds came out. They could see themselves spending more time here.

As Rodney also sings in "Six Days," New Orleans folk "have a weird idea of fun." After a gig in the Big Easy on August 20 (for which they had driven six hours to net twenty-five dollars), he and Reckner decided to accept a couple of punk rock girls' invitation to a party. The others followed Joe's pen pal Hamilton back to his parents' house in Baton Rouge, where they were scheduled to play Jacy's the following night. Rodney and Reckner carried a case of beer into their destination party house, and immediately noticed something was off. For one, there wasn't much in the way of furniture. For two, multiple attack dogs were chained to cinder blocks in the living room—was this place a puppy mill? For three, a pair of dudes with lengthy criminal records got into a bloody fight over four dollars as a pair of *heavily* faded women offered Rodney and Reckner their services. They ducked away from the mayhem, quietly drinking their beer and eventually passing out on the floor around 5:30 a.m. Within an hour, they woke up at gunpoint, being asked by a boyfriend of one of the girls who invited them to get the hell out, in no uncertain terms.

They drove the van into the French Quarter, trying to get their bearings and sneak in some sightseeing before hitting the highway to Baton Rouge. That morning happened to be the biggest gathering of Black Shriners in the country. Following a rousing speech by NAACP leader Benjamin Hooks criticizing the Reagan administration's engagement with South Africa (on the same day the Associated Press reported the right-wing pigeons approving a weapons test in outer space), thousands gathered to watch the parade proceed from Memorial Auditorium around the corner to Canal Street, boxing the duo in. Floating on barely an hour of sleep, Rodney and Reckner were in no condition for clown-fueled pandemonium. They tried escaping the 90 percent humidity in an art gallery, where Reckner was solicited by a lascivious middle-aged woman.

"It may have been the most bizarre twenty-four hours of my life," recalls Reckner. "If Rodney wasn't with me, I would have sworn it was all a dream."

After Baton Rouge, the depleted band toughed their way through the Southeast for another week. Their North Carolina shows both fell through—Charlotte for an alleged power shortage, and Winston-Salem for their venue's alleged embezzlement scheme—so they drove home. They had extant bookings in Columbus and Morgantown, including an optimistic hundred-dollar-netting night at the latter's Underground Railroad on August 29. After Morgantown, they white-knuckled through fog for five hours back to Coatesville, where they all crashed at the Linderman house. They were done. Though Reckner was extremely apologetic about the van, Rodney Sr. was gracious and happy his son had survived.

"Ironically, as we returned home and September rolled around," Dean wrote, "students returned to colleges and the university radio stations began playing the *Big Lizard* album even more. Our music career and the touring adventures were really just beginning. . . . Things got a little better on the road as we got better at it."

Indeed, their near-death experiences and alcoholic nightmares from that first tour inspired them to tighten up their road game, especially if they were going to be full-time musicians. Professionalism. Punctuality. Politeness. They were not by any means straight edge, even drawing circles on their hands to mock the *X*'s on those of Uniform Choice at a California show, but the partying slowed down immensely. For example, on a legendary 1988 tour stop in Naugatuck, Connecticut, the four young guys with a hit record on its way celebrated Dean and Rodney's belated birthday the most decadent way: with a Fudgie the Whale ice cream cake.

Crash Five: Joe
Though he didn't do it by crashing into Dave and Dean while going the wrong way on a cloverleaf exit, Joe did, for a couple of years, drive Rodney's car until he totaled

it. Today, Rodney proudly lives a car-free lifestyle in South Philadelphia, getting around via SEPTA and the kindness of strangers included in their skillfully crafted tour riders.

6. "BIG TIME OPERATOR"
THE DEAD MILKMEN VS. TEXAS

At the conclusion of their 1985 tour, the Dead Milkmen were in a unique position. With an exceedingly patient friend who had fallen into managing them, they did their due diligence and made Golf Pro Music, named for the fellow the "Gorilla Girl" ate in a 1984 Sellersville ska-cording, a legitimate company. Dave Reckner, equipped to deal with the red tape and other such ASCAP minutiae, became the silent fifth member. All lyrical and music authorship, as well as artwork predominantly by Dean, would remain attributed to the Dead Milkmen. There was no space for rock star bullshit, either. They would mix with the crowd and opening bands before gigs. Dave Blood self-identified as an "entertainer," never "musician" on his tax returns. The Milkmen still pointedly say local artists "join" them for shows rather than "open" for them.

The year 1986 would be a long blur that began with recording *Eat Your Paisley!*, promoting and touring it in several legs, and then once that album was out and "The Thing That Only Eats Hippies" was getting marginal traction, ending by recording *Bucky Fellini* in Texas. The Dead Milkmen were now full-time musicians, and they had to get serious.

Paisley!, named as a lark on the jangle-pop underground scene that Dean loved as well as a comment on Dave Blood's picky eating habits (he always removed garnishes and leaned into a fib that mushrooms, which he happened to hate, would kill him), was an early masterpiece of the "college rock" era. Dandrew Stevens, who first heard it as a teenager in the early nineties, still thinks it's flawless. To Joe, Rodney, and Dean, however, it bears all the scars of that "rushed next-album." A lead-off track that Rodney wrote in twenty minutes to prove to Rich Kaufmann that he could ("Where the Tarantula Lives"), spillover tracks from *Big Lizard* (e.g., "Beach Party Vietnam"), a tour-diary song ("Six Days"), and the greatest shocker: a genuine heartbreak song that Rodney wrote for Barbara ("Take Me Apart"). Were the Dead Milkmen already turning *emo* ("emo" having been invented the previous summer in Washington, DC)? Rodney has a more apt way of describing it: "defanged."

The record also reflected a sea change in the American underground. The Replacements had left Twin/Tone for Sire, and independent labels were beginning to behave like majors. A year earlier, the idea of getting a video for "Bitchin' Camaro" on MTV would have been a pipe dream. In March 1986, with Viacom having purchased and optimized programming for advertisers, they launched the indie-specialty show *120 Minutes*. Suddenly, a bunch of jamokes from Philly stood a chance at national viewership. To the labels and management, it meant records, tapes, and (for the rich kids) compact discs flying off shelves. Dave Blood was entranced by the new higher-fidelity format, having experienced a CD player for the first time out in Los Angeles. His bandmates were less enraptured since few in their circles could afford one. For the first CD version of *Big Lizard*, they tacked on lo-fi recordings of "Gorilla Girl" (replete with an announcement Jon Wurster got from Dean's kid neighbor, Zeke) and the audio-collage "Tugena."

"I was very frustrated with both Colin and Enigma because they never got past 'Bitchin' Camaro,'" said Dave Reckner. "I thought we could have worked on [promoting *Big Lizard in My Backyard*] a lot longer, and they had no interest. All they wanted was another record."

"Fortunately for me, and not so much for him, [Dave Reckner] basically did a lot of what a label would actually do for the Milkmen," admits Camerer, "because the record label was basically me and I wasn't really a record label. I was basically a financier."

Unused artwork for a "Tiny Town" seven-inch single.
Courtesy of Dean Sabatino.

Camerer made it clear that if they weren't touring or making a new album, they were setting money on fire. The band joked about pocketing most of the $5,000 advance from Fever and recording the new album during "dark" daytime hours at venue Irving Plaza up in New York, calling it *At Budokan*. They decided to stay local, though, asking John Wicks if he'd like to produce their next record at Third Story's new location in West Philly. Wicks was confused, since what he did for those *Big Lizard* sessions didn't really qualify as "producing." Both parties realized the arrangement had "mistake" written all over it. Punch-in studio trickery was the rage, and Wicks divided the band members up by session, which was anathema to them. Dean, ever the studio prodigy, laid down his tracks quickly. Dave Blood's first "bass day" devolved into a standoff. Wicks told him he needed to record using his fingers—something that he could not physically do. Joe got called in to mediate, convincing Dave to use a fuzzy pick. Wicks did talk the band into cutting off an introduction to "The Thing That Only Eats Hippies." The pop zeitgeist of that year involved kowtowing to people's MTV-decimated attention spans. Accordingly, "Hippies" became the band's first music video, which they filmed (on tape) at Third Story. David Wildmann, who directed, and their pal Chris Coccia made appearances as the hippies. The song even saw release as a seven-inch single . . . in Australia. Liberation Records licensed it due to a cult of fans that 3RRR DJs were helping build in Melbourne.

"They were very popular amongst the teens seeking alternative or punk music," recalls top Aussie fan Justin Daniel. "The tape-trading days of the eighties always had a Milkmen track on them when compilations were passed around. The hugely influential overnight TV music show called *RAGE* used to play their music videos, and tracks could be heard on Triple R radio and nationally on Triple J. A tour, if it happened back [then], would have been well supported and in decent-size venues."

Closing track "The Fez," a Butthole Surfers rip-off (prominently declared by Rodney), was inspired by their "life-changing" opportunity to open for the Texan psychos at the East Side Club on Joe's twenty-second birthday. Though it developed as a lark to test their audience's patience over 1985, playing the song live became a ritual. *The Philadelphia in Love* DVD includes a quintessential "Fez" that ended a 1987 show in St. Louis. Their roadie Jeff Fox plugs in a second guitar to make noise while Rodney spurts non sequiturs like "Give me $6.66 worth of unleaded and make it snappy! I'm driving my granddaughter to the abortion clinic!" As everything collapses, Rodney wrestles Joe's guitar away from him, and Joe announces that "the Dead Milkmen have left the building," before recalling a dream he once had about having breakfast and discussing nuclear power with Dave Blood's favorite pop star, Madonna.

The song's biggest hater, unsurprisingly, was Camerer, who could not help but mentally tabulate the merch sales it cost the band as audience members trickled out the longer "The Fez" went. He made the mistake of verbalizing this concern. The band decided it was going on the next album, with Rodney opening it screaming "HELLO, COLIN!!" It was also a unifying moment; Wicks agreed to let the band record live in the room with each other, since it would have been impossible otherwise. Gibby Haynes would remain in the Milkmen picture: they later roped him in as a guest vocalist on the closing track of *Metaphysical Graffiti*. Two years after that, Gibby lent unhinged guest vocals to Ministry's left-field hit "Jesus Built My Hot Rod"; the Milkmen replied in 1993 with "The Infant of Prague Customized My Van."

Despite the band now having David Reckner to deal with

the unpunk stuff in an official capacity, bigger questions about their future were emerging. Joe's parents tried to pump the brakes. His pending career as a punk rock star gave him a new level of confidence, upon returning from the 1985 tour, he decided to come out to his father. It went horribly. Scarred from his father's Catholic blowback, Joe agreed to "work" on himself. It should have been a liberating time—the scenes they traversed in Philly were defiantly queer, and that floated into the Dead Milkmen. David and Dean, both of svelte figures and comfortable in their sexuality, embraced makeup and cross-dressing—especially once they started making videos. David painted his fingernails, wore dangly jewelry, and as documented in a photo widely spread at his memorial concerts, performed at least once in a full Girl Scout uniform.

"Dave was straight, and he was more feminine than I'll ever be," laughs David's youngest brother Kurt, who spent the eighties and nineties in the closet before coming out in 2002. That same year, in an email interview, Joe Genaro expressed a similar exasperation: "I guess you have to come out over and over again when you are gay. Once just doesn't do it." He had been gradually coming out to friends over the past fifteen years. In 1987, he came out to David, the first of his bandmates. Joe had long assumed incorrectly that his confidant had drawn the conclusion on his own.

"I was taken aback that *he* was taken aback," said Joe recently. "He was concerned that if I came out more broadly, more publicly, that I could put myself in danger, and he was concerned about what Rodney might think and what it would mean for the band. But I had not considered at that point about coming out publicly, and my dad would not have appreciated that, so it did not really matter. But I did decide not to tell Dean or Rodney. I had a feeling Rodney already had his suspicions about me, and I later learned that Dean did not have a clue."

With momentum pulling at the Milkmen in late 1985—complete with another tour out to the Midwest to help finance the studio time for their next record—Joe had been reticent to rock the boat.

"I was robbing Peter to pay Paul just to try to keep a couple of rents paid and some college loans that were due," said Dave Reckner. "We had a meeting and I pushed him and pushed him, [asking] what would make this 'real' for [his parents]. They said, maybe if Joe had health insurance."

Reckner's frustration with Fever was being echoed in his frustration in Philadelphia. He joined forces with David Wildmann, the generously coiffed Kennel Club booker who lived up to his name. The two Davids were "salad dynamics" in extremis. While Reckner fretted over spreadsheets and stage divers, Wildmann was P. T. Barnum, loving the spectacle, the glamour, and company of partners across the gender spectrum. He had been in club management since 1977, when he took over the Rainbow at 1215 Walnut Street. In 1983, he reopened it as the Kennel Club, one of the first Philly venues to blend video and multimedia with live shows, dance nights, and barbecues. They were hosting fundraisers for gay rights groups and youth organizations at the height of the AIDS crisis. He subverted Philly's antiquated authoritarian alcohol laws by arranging all-ages matinees for touring hardcore bands. In 1986, he started Meta Meta Records to release *Fiat Lux*, the sophomore LP by Ruin (whose bassist Cordy Swope would give out his phone number, 557-8252, with the memetic device "KK-SUCK-2").

"There really wasn't anybody that was willing to take a chance promoting Milkmen shows," remembers Reckner of 1986. "The East Side Club had closed a long time ago. The Kennel Club was in the process of closing. It was small, I think three hundred people. We were playing Pi Lam shows and Abe's Steaks, and the live performance situation really sucked."

Joe Genaro with friends at the Kennel Club, 1985. Photo by Chris Coccia.

In October 1984, after leaving YDI, Chuck Meehan discovered a Fellini-esque sandwich shop near UPenn owned by a local Jewish slumlord named Abe, where he began booking eclectic hardcore shows. Meehan later recalled a guy in loud shirts who "always sat [in the front room] drinking coffee and just staring straight ahead . . . he looked like he was real smart, like some weirdo physics genius." The coffee chugger in question was Gary Heidnik, who spent much of 1986 luring young Black women into his cellar. One of Philly's most notorious of America's "serial killer era" inspired Buffalo Bill in Jonathan Demme's 1991 film

The Silence of the Lambs. Meehan also recalled an out-of-sorts young woman arriving to see Circle of Shit play Abe's in 1985, attracted by their liberal use of guns and violent imagery on their flyers. On the day before that Halloween, Sylvia Seegrist would parlay her two months in the army into a shooting spree at the Springfield Mall in Delaware County, killing three people and injuring seven. Like Love Hall, the Elks, and the Hot Club (which also, aptly, burned down) before it, Abe's Steaks was not long for the world.

A series of high-profile murder cases intrigued and terrified the Milkmen. In 1977, one of the cofounders of Earth Day, Ira Einhorn, killed his ex-girlfriend Holly Maddux and composted her body in his closet. The Dead Milkmen would later record their first album in that same building. For Rodney, serial killers would remain an obsession. In a 1994 *Flipside* interview, he mentioned "being up that early [to deliver milk, is] a really bad time to be a serial killer. . . Ted Bundy worked as a milkman for a couple of years and gave it up." He then copped to owning a painting by John Wayne Gacy. On *Pretty Music for Pretty People* in 2014, the Milkmen included an appropriately dark tribute to Mary Ann Cotton, the woman who poisoned multiple children and husbands in Victorian England.

Despite the series of violent events across the city in 1985—the police department's notorious bombing of the MOVE House (and the rest of Osage Avenue) happened one week after the Church of the SubGenius convention—and a seismic strike of sanitation workers that stunk up the city in 1986, things were changing.

"It wasn't really until the Rendell administration, the mayor who changed Philly's political scene from, like, a really corrupt machine to a slightly more functioning government," said Andrew Chalfen. "That was right around the time where the inklings of change were happening."

Reckner and Wildmann formed RAW Ltd., using Wildmann's tiny house near Fourth and Gabriel as office space. Carol Schutzbank, who managed the Electric Love Muffin and Ruin, joined their dream team part-time. Reckner's decision to incorporate temporarily ended his relationship with his parents, who had expected him to join their family research company. Vindication came that fall when RAW had a smash hit out of the gate with Fela Kuti at the sold-out Trocadero. They quickly made one of Philly's best midsize venues into their playground, which it would stay for years, providing a reliable home base for the Milkmen as their audience grew.

Shortly after recording *Paisley!*, the Milkmen used Austin as an anchor for another tour through the South. For a show in San Antonio on February 19, Glass Eye connected them with a seventies cover band called Billy Zygote and the Love Bubbles. Despite the venue's name, Taco Land wisely did not serve food, only a steady stream of whatever the proprietor, Ramiro (known as Ram) Ayala, decided you were going to chug. The whole audience of shit-hammered regulars made it into a party. An older woman named Glinda slurred dirty jokes to Dean before the gig and flashed her panties ("She's got a LOT to share!") while dancing on the pool table during their set. The Love Bubbles lent them their cowboy hats. It was one of the best nights the Dead Milkmen ever had on tour, and they quickly penned a tribute to the Mexican biker bar.

Due to a manufacturing error that Restless didn't catch, at least one shipment of the *Eat Your Paisley!* cassette shipped with the incorrect tape inside, one belonging to Cryptic

Slaughter's thrashtacular debut album *Convicted*. One confused young fan, Ben White, bought the tape at a shop in suburban Virginia.

"It was the first piece of 'adult' music I ever bought for myself," said Ben. "I could tell something was wrong, just based off the cover art and track listing not matching."

Not knowing what else to do, he mailed a letter to the Dead Milkmen PO Box. His letter was one of a flurry of alerts at what had happened to the *Paisley* tape. There was nothing the Dead Milkmen could do, so within a few weeks, Dave Blood wrote him back claiming they were secret KGB operatives. He subscribed Ben to the *DM Newzletter*, which led him to other influential zines like *Maximumrocknroll*. Before long, he was making his own zines. He asked the Dead Milkmen to play Richmond for his sixteenth birthday in 1989. They couldn't, but Dean sent him a card. In his twenties, Ben moved into a punk house called the Snake Pit, and after relocating to Austin, he began a daily diary comic strip called *Snake Pit*. Today, Ben Snakepit still feels like he owes much of his creative life to the Dead Milkmen.

Shortly after *Paisley!* hit stores that summer, the Milkmen opened for the Ramones in Chicago. Soon after that, at a headlining gig at the Ritz Theater in New York, David met a young local with music industry ambitions named Jennifer Lehrer (who would later marry JFA singer Brian Brannon). She was a student at Bennington College, a microscopic liberal arts school buried in the southwestern corner of Vermont. For the next year and a half, whenever the Milkmen were off the road, David would sojourn up to Bennington, occasionally bringing Rodney. As much as the crunchy school's girls were an easy target for Rodney's rants, he loved the scene.

"[David] did a bunch of songwriting [at Bennington]," said Brannon. "He would play music with other friends there. I mean, he was there because he was my boyfriend, but he was pretty self-sufficient at Bennington. He could have happily stayed, and he could have happily gone there. It's funny, when I talk about this to my daughter because age gaps weren't really as big a concern back then. I was very independent, and he wasn't the normal twenty-nine-year-old either. He was in a punk rock band. He wasn't really doing 'establishment' things."

On one visit, Jennifer introduced them to her friend Matt Dubin, and they hit it off quickly. He would later roadie for them at the height of their MTV success, capturing a treasure trove of Super 8 films from the road. He and Rodney would bond over *Kids in the Hall* quotes (later lending the parenthetical "PIG" to their 1995 album title). Jennifer decided to part ways with David by early 1988, but they remained in touch for the rest of his life. She has no memories of any band drama in her time around the Milkmen, likely a by-product of them spreading out socially and reconvening in Philly when business called.

In 1979, the Clash declared that phony Beatlemania had bitten the dust. As 1986 leaned toward 1987, Elvismania was at a fever pitch—both the phony variety on sale at Graceland and the living, breathing tribute embodied by the Dead Milkmen's Restless labelmate Mojo Nixon. The Fox Network, to apply defibrillators to their own *Late Show* after things crashed and burned with Joan Rivers, offered Arsenio Hall a thirteen-week contract. This opened a window through which Mojo Nixon and Skid Roper crawled through onto national television on the tenth anniversary of the King's death (August 16, 1987). The duo bestowed upon everyone in the audience a cheap Elvis mask and torched the place with "Elvis Is Everywhere."

As Mojo added, the only person who had "no Elvis in 'm" was Michael J. Fox, whose head Rodney would call out for onstage during "The Fez" one week later in St. Louis. *Family Ties* had made Fox an easy target; it also made Justine Bateman an object of affection, particularly for Dean, who changed his stage name to Malory [*sic*] shortly after recording *Eat Your Paisley!* Rodney addresses him as Malory in the "Ballroom Blitz"–aping introduction to "The Pit," and the *Newzletter* referenced him as "Mal," but the alter ego didn't stick. The band received a torrent of letters asking who the hell "Malory" was. "Why did you get a different drummer when Dean was such a good drummer?" Dean would quickly revert to "Clean," but his bandmates took it as a cue to spin a roulette wheel of stage names that wouldn't reset until they broke up. By 1988, Joe Jack Talcum became Jasper Thread, named for Jasper Johns and an affinity for the word "thread." Rodney Anonymous swapped out "Cosloy" for "Amadeus" as his middle name. Dave Blood became "Lord Maniac."

In the secular Linderman household, the world was not split into BC and AD, but "BE" and "AE": Elvis was the King who died for our sins that day in 1977, "stoned and fat and wealthy, and sitting on the bowl." Ironically, Groucho Marx died three days after Elvis, in a hospital bed with dignity, and nobody noticed. E pluribus unum? More like e pluribus Elvis. The rock 'n' roll generation—Rodney P. Linderman and Mary Work especially—experienced premium Elvis; their Bastards-of-Young kids got the gelatinous strip mall version via the *'68 Comeback Special*. Still, they couldn't keep the King out of their veins. Even *Moody Blue*, an LP that included Elvis's final studio recordings, done at Graceland and stitched together like Frankenstein's monster, left an impression on young Rodney.

Rodney Anonymous (leaning over railing) sneaks a Dead Milkmen sticker onto Elvis Presley's grave at Graceland, Memphis. October 24, 1986. Photo by Dan Mapp.

In October 1986, the Dead Milkmen, Dan Mapp, and roadie Lee Woulfe made their way across the South after spending a few days with old Coatesville friends on the Florida Gulf Coast. They stopped in Sarasota to track some demos for the new record, mailing them ahead to Austin. On October 24, they found themselves in Arkansas with a day off, deciding to invade Graceland (i.e., politely pay the admission fee). It felt exactly like Disney World, another common Linderman family vacation destination. Rodney threw a Dead Milkmen sticker down on Elvis's grave as hordes of Japanese tourists snapped his photo. He was not surprised at the crass commercialism of Graceland, but the mob conservatism of the other guests was jarring. He nearly got into a fight with some rednecks who overheard a joke he made about Elvis's well-documented drug problems.

One month later, their tour routed them down the California coast as Thanksgiving approached. On the holiday, they rolled up to Mojo Nixon's place in San Diego, where he greeted them warmly with a stack of Swanson turkey TV dinners and an unending supply of Foster's beer. The timing could not have been better—the road was getting to the Milkmen. Dean and Rodney scuffled, but David broke things up before they exchanged blows. Mojo's girlfriend's three-year-old son regaled them with his song "I Like to Fart," falling off his mini drum kit as a finale. It's inconclusive whether Dean took notes.

"EYYYY! IT'S THE DEAD MILK-MIDGETS!" bellowed Mojo whenever in the presence of his diminutive labelmates. Wherever he went, he was used to being the center of attention; with Rodney, he met his match. They spent hours talking about rockabilly, Elvis, and McDonald's— three subjects Mojo slid into every conversation. In May 1987, he theorized to *Rip* magazine that Ronald McDonald and Ronald Reagan were the same dude, sharing a story about how he and Skid Roper had seen Jesus building a cross out of telephone poles from a McDonald's on Santa Monica Boulevard. Nixon then announced his plans to own the first McDonald's on the moon, where "Klingons, Vulcans, Romulans, and Elvis impersonators" could enjoy Big Macs. As overwhelming as he could be, the Dead Milkmen were enamored with their sideburned labelmate. Joe and David even added a verse to the Ornamental Wigwam song "Punk Rock Girl" in tribute.

One week later, the Dead Milkmen pulled into Austin.

It was after 2 a.m., but Brian Beattie was so excited to begin recording, they listened to the full Sarasota demo tape before he let them go to bed. Their initial sessions for *Bucky Fellini* encountered some friction between Beattie and Dean, who had breezed through the John Wicks sessions.

"Up until then, I don't think we had done any preproduction with a producer," said Dean. "When you've been playing a song for a while in a certain way, it's always a little bit jarring to have somebody tell you, 'Well, can you just do this instead?' So, you just have to adjust. And eventually I came around."

"Philadelphia always understood us," said Beattie, who grew up in the New York catchment of southern Connecticut, releasing singles with his high school bands Tapeworm and Safety Patrol as punk blew up. The interlocking lure of the bohemian life and a lovely, talented classmate named Kathy McCarty (later known as K.) led him to Austin in 1979. His romantic ambitions didn't work out, but the two became lifelong friends and collaborators. By early 1981, Beattie was renting a house near downtown Austin for $150 per month with jobs at Dunkin' Donuts and a new supermarket called Whole Foods. In 1983, he and Kathy, who left Buffalo Gals, assembled Glass Eye. In 1985, they toured back up to the Northeast, stopping in Philly to play the Pi Lam Human Barbecue at UPenn, quickly melding minds with the Milkmen. Passing out on the couch in the Milkmen's basement, Beattie's mind was blown hearing "Bitchin' Camaro" for the first time. Brian passed Joe Jack two tapes by an inimitable Austin singer-songwriter named Daniel Johnston—*Yip/Jump Music* and *Hi, How Are You*—both of which blew his mind. "I think Daniel and I had parallel lives in a lot of ways," said Joe.

The first strength in their collaboration was how Beattie was, by most accounts, as weird as the Dead Milkmen. For their next three albums—the "Texas Trilogy"—Beattie would typically encourage every left-field-to-insane decision the band made. A song with no guitars, built around a drum machine? Putting *actual* violins and accordions on the track? Sending Dean and his kit to a different place like Martin Hannett allegedly did with Joy Division? Interspersing improvised (and increasingly offensive) anecdotes about maggot farms and the anti-Semitic remarks of Public Enemy's Professor Griff to utilize every inch of tape? A love letter to Sha Na Na? Free-range guest vocals by Gibby Haynes? What's the title "Anderson, Walkman, Buttholes and How!" referencing, anyway? The answer to all these questions is yes. Beattie also encouraged the band to give him a new nickname for each record. They chose "Mud Lounge" as a play on Mutt Lange, "Orchid Breath" for the sexual innuendo, and "Bong Wizard" for *Metaphysical Graffiti* because it "was just too brilliant not to use." He used the term "Beelzebubba" as a nickname he had "for a certain type of personality" on occasion, which was also too good not to use.

The second strength was how mutually beneficial the budding collaboration was. The Dead Milkmen were a highly literate, radical band often written off as "unserious." Glass Eye were a fun-loving, creative band often written off as (an unfortunately ubiquitous term at the time) "art fags." *Bucky Fellini* would represent a full-on infection by both Glass Eye and the Lone Star State. Though "Jellyfish Heaven" may have fit on *Paisley!*, "Watching Scotty Die," "Big Time Operator," and especially "Instant Club Hit (You'll Dance to Anything)" could only have been willed into existence with the arsenal that Glass Eye provided.

Bucky Fellini was conceived to suggest a "Texas surrealist filmmaker," a tribute to the art-house films the band loved—the more *giallo*, the better. A reference to Dario Argento's *Profondo Rosso* (1977) sits on the cover. The Italian auteur Federico Fellini's movies like *La Dolce Vita* (1960) and *8½* (1963) were wild meta commentaries on journalism and filmmaking, respectively, that incorporated eclectic casts of characters. The Dead Milkmen's songs and albums were unhinged commentaries on punk and politics that also incorporated eclectic casts of characters (both real and imagined).

While preparing to record *Bucky*, Joe, Dean, Dan Mapp, and Lee Woulfe caught *Blue Velvet* at the Dobie (skipping the midnight Three Stooges film fest). They had been too drunk to appreciate *Dune* at a drive-in in California the previous summer, but Lynch's surrealism hit just right this time. "Very good, very disturbing movie," wrote Dean. "David Lynch directs, *Eraserhead* style, yet refined and able to tell a story." For years, Rodney would occasionally scream profane quotes onstage by Dennis Hopper's psychopath Frank Booth. "DON'T YOU FUCKIN' LOOK AT ME!" Fellini's influence on David Lynch, whose artistic life began in Philadelphia, was unquestionable. Lynch's first film, presented in 1967, was a one-minute loop projected onto the wall at the Pennsylvania Academy of the Fine Arts called *Six Men Getting Sick*. Lynch had also happened to live at Thirteenth and Wood Streets, a block away from 1316 Callowhill, where America's first serial killer H. H. Holmes set up a phony patent office with, and then burned alive, fellow con artist Benjamin Pitezel in 1894. Philadelphians affectionately refer to this as the "Eraserhood." Lynch didn't shoot *Eraserhead* there, but his 1977 midnight movie put on full display the neighborhood's reach into his psyche. On his paradigm-shifting TV series *Twin Peaks*, both agent Dale Cooper (Kyle MacLachlan) and his unseen (until the *Return* series) associate Diane Evans (Laura Dern) were from Philadelphia. Underground Arts, a subterranean club at Twelfth and Callowhill, became a preferred local venue for the reconstituted Dead Milkmen in the 2010s, with Dandrew often playing in his Laura Palmer T-shirt. In 2014, Rodney mixed *Eraserhead* with his appreciation for gritty German expressionism to storyboard a Murnau-style video for "The Sun Turns Our Patio into a Lifeless Hell."

In mid-eighties Austin, Fellini's work was also massaging the brains of University of Texas filmmakers like Richard Linklater, who would help elevate Austin to indie film sanctity in 1990 with his own Texas-fried *8½*, which he called *Slacker*. In 1985, Linklater was filming local DIY festivals like Woodshock, capturing the city's insurgent counterculture—including their buddy Daniel Johnston—right around the time that MTV came calling and threatened the scene's splendid isolation. Glass Eye's national "break" came on an episode of MTV's short-lived *Cutting Edge* on August 25, 1985. The episode also featured Daniel Johnston backed up by pub-rock chameleons the Rhythm Rats. Millions of curious music fans watched around the country, including the Dead Milkmen, who raced home from North Carolina to catch the episode at the Lindermans' in Coatesville.

Austin had long been the "live music capital of the world," but now it was a hell of a time to be in any local band. Bar bands like the Fabulous Thunderbirds rode an iconic video for "Tuff Enuff" to platinum sales. Even local favorites like the LeRoi Brothers, founded by former

Thunderbird Mike Buck, enjoyed the windfall, with their album *Open All Night* hitting the *Billboard* 200. Like most bar bands, their repertoire mixed originals with regional covers. The latter included "Big Time Operator," a 1959 recording by Dale Houston, a nineteen-year-old minister's son from Collins, Mississippi. It leapt out at Buck and his bandmates from side B of *Louisiana Swamp Pop*, a 1977 compilation issued and exported by the UK collector label Flyright. The album's inclusion of the Big Bopper's first recording ("Boogie Woogie") may have been the selling point, but "Big Time Operator" earned a spot on the LeRoi Brothers' set in 1981. Six years later at a studio in nearby San Marcos, the Milkmen's resident classic rock dude, Dave Blood, brought the song to the group.

"[I] never met Dave, although [we] loved their version with references to our pals Stevie and Charlie," said Buck, unfazed at Rodney's improvised proclamation that Stevie Ray Vaughan and Charlie Sexton were "cheesy Texas motherfuckers." The moment was unforgettable for Beattie, who unlike Wicks, enthusiastically let Rodney sing live in the studio over his bandmates. He was obsessed with the magic of those first takes.

"I had aesthetic problems with really clean, shiny-sounding recording," said Beattie. "And I am surprised to see that people were talking about them being kind of more clean sounding. But that's not what I thought was going on."

In the early spring, they chose to make a video for their cover of "Big Time Operator," their first collaboration with director Adam Bernstein, the go-to guy for They Might Be Giants.

"Music videos [were] a wide-open laboratory; it was like the children's crusade," said Bernstein of his early era. "There was no supervision. They would give me $30,000, $50,000, and you would disappear for a weekend to shoot a video. . . . The Dead Milkmen would say that they like the films of Dario Argento, [so the videos became] a laboratory for trying out visual effects or trying out a piece of equipment."

Despite their misgivings with WMMR, they invited Cyndy Drue, whose show "Street Beat" advocated for them, up to the Bronx to play one of the dancing nurses who flanked Rodney's FrankenElvis character.

Behind the scenes at the "Big Time Operator" video shoot, directed by Adam Bernstein (standing at wheelchair), Bronx, NY, 1987. Courtesy of Cyndy Drue.

"I'm in Screen Actors Guild [now] and everything, but I didn't bring that up with the Milkmen," said Cyndy. "Of course they didn't pay me, but that's okay . . . I just remember it being very fun and very organized—the director knew what he was doing, and it didn't take forever to get the takes."

As was becoming tradition, Joe sang lead on two tracks,

one of which was "Watching Scotty Die," the folk jam he and Dave Blood had cowritten four years prior. Until they were deep in the heart of Texas, with K. McCarty's bleeding violin at their disposal, the song had no prayer of crossing over to the Dead Milkmen. But now, all bets were off. The other song Joe sang was a cover of Daniel Johnston's "Rocketship." He was anxious about what Daniel thought, convinced that his cosmic counterpart disliked it.

"That's probably all my fault because right after [*Bucky Fellini*] came out, I played it for Daniel," said Beattie, "and he [noticed] they changed it a little bit right in the beginning. That's the first thing Daniel heard. Years later, he just loved it and I made probably a tragic mistake telling Joe that Daniel said that, because years later he still held it in his heart that Daniel didn't like it."

Six years later, after pictures of Kurt Cobain wearing a shirt with Johnston's art circulated, McCarty recorded a version of "Rocketship" (with Beattie doing the countdown) on *Dead Dog's Eyeball*, an LP of radio-ready Daniel Johnston covers. In early 2020, following Daniel's death the prior September, Joe Jack Talcum performed a full set of covers following a screening of *The Devil and Daniel Johnston* at World Cafe Live. He still regularly includes "True Love Will Find You in the End," "Living Life," and "Big Business Monkey" in his solo acoustic sets.

Ironically, where Rodney would have barely anything to do with "Punk Rock Girl" a year later, Joe had very little to do with "Instant Club Hit," one of the few songs in the Milkmen catalog with no guitars. Joe's only contribution was swinging a voopy noisemaker along with Dave Reckner's power saw. The lyrics were mostly one-liners Rodney claimed to overhear at a goth club in Amarillo.

Beattie and engineer Mike Stewart were on board when Rodney presented that beat on his drum machine. They sampled their roadie Lee Woulfe saying "art fag," chopping it through the breakdown portion; whenever they played the song live on the *Bucky* tour, it was interpolated as a medley with "Swordfish," omitting the bells, whistles, and slurs. In the studio, McCarty, Sheri Lane, and Kim Cook provided the Milkmen with their first backup singers. It isn't enough to say that "Instant Club Hit" is unique within the Dead Milkmen catalog; nothing else from that era sounds remotely like it. If the single came out on SoundCloud in the 2020s, it would be billed as "DMxGlassEye."

In the studio recording "Instant Club Hit (You'll Dance to Anything)" in San Marcos, Texas. (L–R): Dave Blood, K. McCarty, Brian Beattie, Joe Jack Talcum, Mike Stewart. Photo by Dan Mapp.

Fever and Enigma agreed to release "Instant Club Hit" as a twelve-inch single. David Wildmann oversaw two remixes: the "Hung Like a Horse" mix and an isolated instrumental called "Boner Beats." The real treat, however, is the inclusion of a studio rendition of "Ask Me to Dance," a foundational Baker Street Blood-Talcum composition. It also included the only vinyl appearances of "Tugena" and "Vince Lombardi Service Center," an instrumental that began life as a sound-check jam called "Hü Dü."

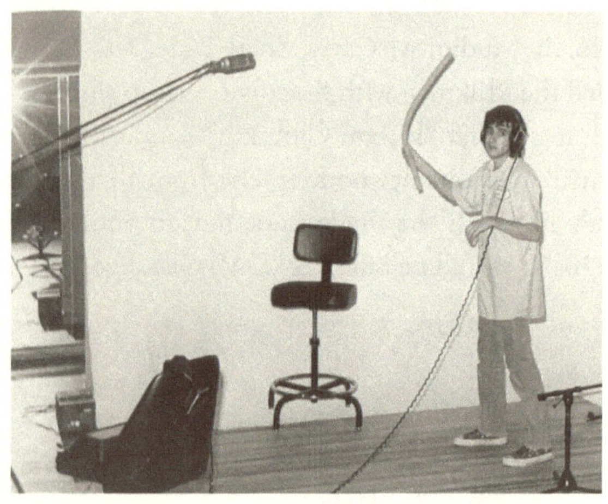

Joe Jack Talcum adds noise to "Instant Club Hit (You'll Dance to Anything)" at the Fire Station, San Marcos, Texas, December 1986. Photo by Dan Mapp.

As the nineties arrived and both the Milkmen and Mojo found themselves marginalized by a changing industry, they remained rocks for one another. As Rodney loudly channeled Mojo on "Smokin' Banana Peels" (sample lyric: "TALK TO ME ABOUT ELVIS"), Enigma issued "Smokin'" as a single and filmed a video in the California desert, and the Milkmen dropped in for an appearance on Mojo's video for "(619) 239-KING." It was too pure a marriage, and to both, the moment of being able to set the building on fire from inside was fleeting. In late 1990, Mojo, the Milkmen, and the Cave Dogs joined forces for the "Amuck in America" tour—a twenty-three-date romp sponsored by Fujifilm, making it the Milkmen's best-documented tour of the analog era. Fujifilm printed in-concert programs, including the full Milkmen back catalog, pull-down quotes by the likes of Robert Christgau and Jim Walewander, and teasing "future releases [that] include a home video, a vacation guidebook, and a van repair manual."

The following spring, while the Dead Milkmen were negotiating their new contract with Hollywood Records, they went to see Mojo and his band the Toad Lickers, where he improvised a parody of "Methodist Coloring Book" about how short they all were. In 1995, Rodney jumped onstage to sing backup for Mojo in exchange for a steady stream of free shots. Twenty years later, the Dead Milkmen finally returned to San Diego, playing the Belly Up club. In the face of accelerating health problems, Mojo catapulted onstage in the middle of "Punk Rock Girl" to FEEEEL THE POWER right as Joe sang the line about him. The crowd went berserk.

"After the show it was this incredible verbal ping-pong match with Rodney and Mojo cracking each other and everyone else up," recalls Dandrew.

Mojo continued performing and hosting specialized rock 'n' roll programming like "Lyin' Cocksuckers" on SiriusXM. In February 2024, aboard the Outlaw Country Cruise in Puerto Rico, Mojo's heart finally caught up with him. Like the Milkmen, whom he remained close with until the end of his life, he had a dalliance with mainstream success, but he refused to let it change him or let the bastards grind him down. Elvis is still everywhere.

7. "PUNK ROCK GIRL"
THE DEAD MILKMEN VS. MTV

As the eighties melted into the nineties, while MTV was overflowing with focus-grouped metal and pop, "Punk Rock Girl" broke out of the *120 Minutes* ghetto, hinting that pop music fans were ready for something alternative. Released in the heart of when such things were quantifiable, "Punk Rock Girl" made it to No. 11 on *Billboard*'s (then months-old) "Alternative Airplay" Top 40 chart. It pushed *Beelzebubba* to No. 101 on the *Billboard* 200, sixty-two spaces higher than *Bucky*'s peak.

"I was convinced we had a hit," says Dave Reckner, "and I was right."

Some hold firm that the Dead Milkmen undermined their career by refusing to mime "Punk Rock Girl," bombarding the dance floor with rubber worms, and handcuffing Downtown Julie Brown in their appearance on *Club MTV*. It's equally likely that the Dead Milkmen are the only reason anybody *remembers* that show. The Milkmen's appearance represented their apex of mainstream fame, a completely inane moment of anarchy they had earned for themselves. They were also guest stars with Kevin Seal on the more culturally appropriate (for them) *120 Minutes*, and they still took the piss out of college rock, improvising a song about saving the rainforest and playing the "Banana Peels" B-side "The Puking Song." Also, Dave Blood (then still going by "Lord Maniac") told Seal his name was Lyndon LaRouche and his favorite color was "clear, man."

The story of "Punk Rock Girl" was as much the Dead Milkmen's commercial peak as a cautionary tale about the dynamics of "success" ruining everything. There's much to be celebrated: South Street (namely the Philadelphia Pizza Company and Zipperhead) was now on national TV, elevating the band to ur-celebrity status, and slotting the Dead Milkmen into karaoke catalogs worldwide. In the wake of a dark year that saw the death of a mentor, it became a personal and professional validation. It also set off a series of events that revealed, and kicked, multiple hornets' nests, bringing the band to the brink of collapse. For a wide array of reasons, they managed to push through and continue another five years, knowing full well that just like they'd never outrun the "Bitchin' Camaro," they would never get over the "Punk Rock Girl."

"The record company doesn't pay enough attention to you until you have a hit, and then they pay too much attention to you," said Joe Jack Talcum.

Even before the video landed on major rotation on MTV, things were heating up. *Bucky Fellini* had blipped in the *Billboard* 200, and Enigma had a feeling about this next one. They threw a raucous release party for *Beelzebubba*, renting out a bowling alley in New Jersey where everyone got hammered. On December 9, 1988, the Milkmen played an early album release show at the Theatre of the Living Arts on South Street, then ended the night at the Palladium in Midtown Manhattan for the anniversary party for *Spin* magazine (whose writer Chuck Eddy had shit on them at least once by that point).

"The *Spin* party was stressful and stupid, but I did get Enigma to pay for the helicopter," says Reckner.

According to members of the band Dead Milkmen, the library is a "great place to pick up chicks." That was one of the testimonials to the advantages of literacy and visits to the library during the "Rock, Rap n' Read" program before ninth graders at the main branch of the Free Library. That's Robert Palestini (left), superintendent of schools for the Archdiocese of Philadelphia, listening as the Dead Milkmen spoke to the kids. (And you can imagine, Catholic school teachers were muttering to themselves, "A great place to pick up chicks?!!")

From The Philadelphia Inquirer, October 10, 1988.

The origins of "Punk Rock Girl" predate the real Dead Milkmen by a year or two, when Genaro got his job shelving books at the Temple University library. He remembers bandying about the idea of a "punk rock nursery rhyme" set on South Street. When he and David began writing songs together in early 1982, it would show up during jam sessions. After "Bitchin' Camaro" gained traction and the Dead Milkmen was now their job, the Ornamental Wigwam became a canvas for ideas that didn't fit with Rodney's and Dean's contributions. Occasionally, they would literally become a canvas, donning white robes in front of a screen, upon which their friend Jay Schwartz would project 16 mm films from his collection.

The story was a conceptual narrative of a naive suburban kid who falls for his ideal "punk rock girl." The opening line, "One Saturday I took a walk to Zipperhead," one of the most iconic of eighties punk, reflected a typical activity for a suburban kid intrigued by the counterculture. Although Zipperhead's owner Rick Millan closed it in 2005, the shop remains (with some help from the Milkmen) seared into public memory, around the corner from former partner Stef Jolles's shop Crash Bang Boom, which she opened that year. For a 2018 episode of the eighties-nostalgia flagship sitcom *The Goldbergs*, a suburban dork goes kicking shit on South Street to impress his newly punk girlfriend; Millan's daughter, Tedra, showed up as a clerk. The song also includes a pivotal scene at the Philadelphia Pizza Company, which the band would use as a rendezvous point, a safe harbor in a changing neighborhood as they came of age. Their character also cites "California Dreamin'" as a Beach Boys song—both a time stamp of the Beach Boys' anemic, forgotten 1986 cover version and a world-building facet of the narrator's ignorance.

In 1987, while Joe and David were workshopping "Punk Rock Girl" up and down South Street, David Wildmann learned distressing news about his health. Coupled with Carol Schutzbank's long-standing heart problems, he and Reckner decided it may be wise to bring somebody else into the RAW family. That October, they invited Michigander Howard Kramer—another friend of Dave Blood's from those first tours—to size Philly up.

"I had never been to Philadelphia before, and I drove out in my little Toyota and spent the weekend with Dave and Dave," said Kramer. "I remember them walking me down South Street. It was very funny, them trying to make Philly sound pretty happening at the time. They're like, 'Oh yeah . . . Mark Goodman from MTV!' He was a DJ in Philadelphia."

That moment, Goodman himself walked out of a trendy boutique and passed the three of them, his Jew-fro bouncing in the breeze. They knew he had lived in New York since 1981, but the kismet moment solidified Kramer's decision to accept RAW's offer. There was only so much he could do between Ann Arbor and Detroit in this, the year of *RoboCop*.

At an Ornamental Wigwam set at Bacchanal, Joe recalls audience members encouraging the duo to turn "Punk Rock Girl" into a Dead Milkmen song. They initially balked. It was too "cutesy," heavily influenced by Joe's resurgent attempt to collect the children's records of his youth. By May of 1988, however, the song was fully integrated into the Dead Milkmen's set at the Chestnut Cabaret, supported by a touring Glass Eye. The band made plans to return to Austin that July to make another record.

Within a few weeks, tragedy struck. On June 2, David Wildmann died of complications from AIDS. His obituary in the *Inquirer* said it was cancer. "Life Is Shit," the powerhouse closing track on *Beelzebubba*, became the Dead Milkmen's way of saying goodbye. It grew into a staple of the band's live sets and a first-ballot Hall of Fame diagram of what set the Milkmen apart as they hit their commercial peak: gallows humor that was crudely optimistic and sentimental, laced with references to Richard Nixon, Schoolly D, and Bob

Crane. This was life as they knew it.

"[David] was a beloved character in the scene, having been a DJ, and he taught me and Reckner a lot," Kramer recalled. "He had this phrase that 'a nightclub should never be more than 80 percent complete,' because you should always be working on something where it'll bring people back in, because the next time they come, it'll be different."

"At the time, Rodney had a love-hate relationship with being out in front as the crowds got bigger," said Reckner. "He is very funny and loud, but he's also incredibly mischievous and doesn't mind punishing the audience if it suits him. That's the dark side that I think David [Wildmann] worked on."

Rodney held Wildmann in especially high regard. Both were avid showmen, and they had developed a strong rapport, often providing external support for the singer. Suffice it to say, Rodney would really have liked to have Wildmann around, given what was about to happen.

Back in Texas that summer, the *Beelzebubba* sessions were typical Austin fun, but things started getting weird. The band wanted to continue exploring the Glass Eye arsenal, including keyboards, which Joe would play (credited in the liner notes as "Bucky Fellini"). For "Punk Rock Girl," the decision to forgo the synthesizer for an actual accordion is still smoldering.

"I had two [accordions]," Beattie recalls. "We had one in Glass Eye, and I owned one of my own. I knew how to construct chords, and I could vaguely play it, but I wasn't like a real accordion player."

Despite a surge of popularity in the Mario Lanza party-records era of the sixties—both Tony Genaro and Rodney Linderman Sr. played accordion as their sons grew up—the instrument had become a hokey punch line to the Bastards of Young. Suddenly, via Weird Al and They Might Be Giants, the accordion was getting countercultural again. Rodney suggested he was willing to break his "No Accordions" rule, especially now that they were in cahoots with TMBG's video director.

"[Rodney] was joking around about it," recalled Beattie. "The next thing I remember was that Joe picked up the accordion, and immediately, not only did he have facility with the melody side, but he was doing the bass and chords on the button side. I remember Rodney just looking at Joe and saying, 'Joe's Italian heritage is coming right out! Just listen to that, it's like we're in an Italian restaurant!' He was looking at it with real awe, because he knew that Joe had just picked it up."

When it became evident how much weight Enigma and Reckner were putting on this song, Rodney felt boxed out again. It was that moment back in 1982, when he was marooned in West Chester while Joe and Dave were jamming in Philly, and writing to Joe, assuring him he was becoming a better drummer.

"I think the record company would have been happy if I'd had an accident shortly after that and gone away," Rodney told *Razorcake*. "I've had this inferiority complex that I'm always sure that our manager would be happy if I had an accident and Joe sang all the time."

On the third weekend of October 1988, the band, Adam Bernstein, and a bunch of well-wishers gathered at the decrepit Eastern State Penitentiary. Like hardcore shows of yore at Love Hall, this was a "black booger" shoot.

They set up adjacent to the cell where Al Capone stayed in 1929. The prison was years away from OSHA-grade safety for visitors; Dean had to switch to his brushes, as standard snare hits would dislodge chunks of ancient plaster from the ceiling. Their friend Miriam, who played in a mythical New York band called God's Crotch, came down to play the titular, mohawked love interest. Dave Blood made two different appearances in drag: as the girl's Pepsodent-smiling mother and the hot-tea-refusing server at the Philly Pizza Co. Waitress Dave appeared again at the end of the video, peering in from the back of his friend Kenn Kweder's station wagon. David would reprise his drag role as a go-go dancer in "Smokin' Banana Peels" that spring. Allegedly, he was skinny enough, and dolled up enough, that members of Bernstein's crew ogled him when he emerged from the dressing room.

That spring, Enigma's correspondent Caprice Carmona delivered the tape to MTV studios, and thanks to a full-court press by the label (who allegedly hired interns to call MTV around the clock to request it), the video started doing well. The Milkmen were suddenly this hot commodity for the video networks, and their shows started getting noticeably louder and rowdier. When they weren't on the road, things started getting ugly as David's anxiety over money reared its head.

"I think that was mostly due to his girlfriend at the time," begins Joe, "but she and then Dave—after 'Punk Rock Girl' was a hit—suspected someone of skimming money or stealing because they were wondering, 'Well, where did all this money go?' And I started feeling like they were accusing our manager, then I started feeling that I was getting accused as well."

David called the Philadelphia Art Alliance, who provided a pro bono lawyer. Things came to an impasse. In mid-1989, the band was in a rare position of strength as they negotiated a new deal for a fifth record and beyond. Their contracts with Dave Reckner and Fever/Enigma/Restless were both expiring. Though Reckner had formed RAW Ltd. as a distinct entity, he and the four Dead Milkmen had signed a deal whereby he was, ostensibly, the fifth member. As things were devolving, it took Wes Hein of Enigma to step in and deliver an ultimatum.

"They were gonna get re-signed, and Dave was convinced I was ripping them off," said Reckner. "Wes Hein saved my relationship. He flew out from Los Angeles and basically told the [lawyer] that if I wasn't involved, that there wasn't a deal and he could go fuck himself."

The band then hired Bill Hoffman, a semi-retired tax accountant wholly unfamiliar with their enterprise. All Reckner and Genaro remember was him feeding David's anxiety.

"[Reckner] created RAW Ltd. so he could manage other bands, but we were always under the impression that we were special [and it] was just his side gig, but it really wasn't just his side gig." Genaro continued, "And then he wanted to get out of our partnership and make the same kind of relationship that RAW had with the other artists, and that's eventually what happened. But it was a rocky road to get there."

When the smoke cleared, Dave Blood got his way and the Dead Milkmen formed an S corp, where the four of them shared publishing rights and finances. Unable to use the word "dead" in a company registered in the Commonwealth of Pennsylvania, they abbreviated it to DM Music.

"Eventually, it all worked out," Reckner reflects, "but yeah, it was ugly."

Joe, still operating publicly as Jasper Thread, retreated into a panoply of distractions, deciding to change his name again. Alex Liss, a Beatlemaniac theater kid Joe knew, gave him the name Butterfly Fairweather. Not on comfortable speaking terms with David, Rodney swirling in a sea of doubt and alcohol, and Dean's wedding to artist Melissa Bell rightfully occupying him, Joe shifted his emotional energy to another solo tape and a flood of younger pen pals. One of them, a young journeyman who called himself Seven Morris, first saw Joe play at the Cannery in Nashville, where the Milkmen opened for Living Colour.

Joe, Dave, and Rodney after landing at Honolulu airport, April 1989.
Courtesy of Dan Mapp.

"I was just mesmerized by his playing, his style," said Morris. "I just watched him the entire time, so I felt compelled to write. I wrote to the band, him specifically, and, lo and behold, to my surprise, he wrote back. So we just corresponded for a bit.

The following year, Morris's family relocated yet again, to rural Floyd, Virginia. It was close enough to Blacksburg, where Joe's literary friend Richie Abowitz was in school, that he came to visit Seven, and they jammed a bit. Given the tension with his collaborators back in Philly, including a depleted songwriting partnership with David, Joe was excited for a clean slate. In Blacksburg, Richie's girlfriend suggested they visit the local "touch-me zoo." They knew two things: one, she meant "petting zoo," and two, their new project had a name.

Rodney and Dave with fans at a signing in Honolulu, April 1989.
Photo by Dan Mapp.

Halvin' My Baby, a solo tape Joe recorded as Butterfly Fairweather, acted like a catalog for his struggle with coming out, especially now that he was the star of a hit MTV video that was, although fictionally, written about a girl.

"I was starting to come out to people," he said. "I was

now at that point in the late eighties, realizing that it's just me and there's nothing I can do about it."

At a late April show in Los Angeles, he befriended a girl named Rebecca who had a clear crush on him.

"She was just in high school, and that's inappropriate," he reflects, though in 1989, it became easier to allow people to assume they were an item than reveal the full truth. Either way, Rebecca's mother felt it was very inappropriate. She left a message on Joe's answering machine threatening legal action if he continued corresponding with her daughter. He sampled the message into a song named for his friend. This wasn't his first time shrugging off a "scandal" like this. *Halvin' My Baby* contained a few other concept songs about apocryphal relationships with women, such as "And Then She Dumped Me," and one about a "girlfriend who threw a brick at his head" called "Don't Do This to Me, Baby." By 1993, he would perform the song with Dean and Andy Bresnan's Big Mess Orchestra, swapping in "boyfriend." He, Sabatino, and Bresnan would finally record an "official" release of the song (in that form) in 1999 as the project Butterfly Joe.

For several reasons—only one of which was the fallout that came from it—the band still refuses to put "Punk Rock Girl" on any pedestal. When they reunited to memorialize Dave Blood in 2004, they took to the stage at the Trocadero and, without uttering a word, kicked off their set with it. Rodney stood behind his keyboard with arms crossed. It was the first time they'd played together in a decade, and every person in the room wanted to hear it, so it was time to get it over with. The crowd sang louder than Joe, even correcting him when he flubbed a lyric in the second verse. It also pulled something into focus: the "casual fans" that their

MTV exposure had attracted in 1989 were gone. Everybody in the room was just as excited to sway and sing along to "Life Is Shit" as anything. The Milkmen had no plans to play more gigs after that weekend, but the distance helped them realize that, despite everything, they had something special with "Punk Rock Girl."

After the S corp was formed, the dust settled, and Rodney needed to set a few things straight. The band had been drowning in the wrong kind of attention all year. As they began plotting out their third Texas album, they wanted to avoid getting so consistently labeled as "wacky." The fictional Dead Milkmen backstory provided a respite for Rodney as his 1989 devolved into a vortex of depression and resentment. Though his childhood drumming and banjo lessons hadn't really stuck, he clung to his Yamaha DX11 as a way forward. One drunken weekend, he, his girlfriend, and some friends made a tape called *20,000 Bong Hits from Home* as the Sunflower Children of God. It was Rodney's stab at his own *Yip/Jump*. Most importantly, he was becoming less dependent on Joe, Dave, and Dean to write music for his lyrics. This was his. One of his songs was an answer-track to Butterfly Fairweather's "If You Love Someone, Set Them Free" called "If You Love Somebody, Set Them on Fire." When Joe heard it, he knew it had to be a Dead Milkmen song. Because Rodney had already built it around a ska rhythm, the full band built a two-tone tune around it. During the *Metaphysical Graffiti* sessions, the band recorded a cover of the Specials' version of Dandy Livingstone's "A Message to You, Rudy" that surfaced thirteen years later on *Now We Are 20*. Naturally, with the eyes of the emerging "alternative" music world upon them, their follow-up to *Beelzebubba* would be composed of one insane decision after another.

For reasons (arguably) related to Enigma Records folding into Capital during promotion, *Metaphysical Graffiti*—inspired by repeated marveled viewings of *The Song Remains the Same* on tour in 1989—was the first LP they released that hadn't outsold the previous one. It was an unquestionable turning point for the band, musically and interpersonally, a challenge they made to themselves to see whether their truce after 1989 would hold. It's still Joe Jack Talcum's favorite record they ever did, despite his eternal grudge over "Methodist Coloring Book." The video featured a series of shots of model buildings being destroyed, one of which was a church. Word got back that MTV wouldn't accept that, so Bernstein decided to reverse the shot, putting the model church back together. It was a minor inconvenience, but it ran antithetical to the spirit of the song.

"I'm still so mad they made us do a video for that song. I didn't even think I was going to be the one to sing it," admits Joe. "I sang it purposefully bad! They used the first take anyway. I treated it like a scratch vocal, because that's what I thought it was."

The original plan was for Joe to continue with his two songs per record. In this case, the songs were the frenetic "I Hate You, I Love You" and the ethereal "Dollar Signs in Her Eyes," a ballad he admits was a pronoun-swapping of his guilt over the dollar signs in his own eyes after "Punk Rock Girl."

"They wanted to be a little more 'prog,'" recalls Brian Beattie as the Milkmen reassembled in Austin with the ambitious nod to "Another Brick in the Wall" that starts the record. Beattie had heard that "beige sunshine" was a potent strain of acid that had allegedly once circulated Austin. It was also inspired by Rodney's Sunflower tracks "Cobalt Blue Sunshine" and "The Sun Shines Out of My Asshole." When Beattie decided to go full Floyd and incorporate a chorus of kids, a phone chain assembled. His friend Michael Baggett had two sons, Heron and Tyrone, who would be on board. Tyrone called his best friend Graham Williams, who was the biggest Milkmen fan in their sixth-grade class. Mike Sullivan's daughters Julia and Sarah were fixtures at Arlyn Studios; when they were in fourth and sixth grade, they made a (faint) cameo on *Beelzebubba*, screaming "We're from upstairs!" at the beginning of "Bad Party." They also recruited engineer Stuart Sullivan's daughter Helen, along with five others with parents in the scene.

Joe took some convincing after an offhanded remark Beattie made that the finale of "Punk Rock Girl" recalled the Sherman Brother's ubiquitous 1964 Disney anthem, "It's a Small World." Whether it was exhaustion or taken as a personal jab, Joe snapped. "NO! It does NOT sound like 'It's a Small World!'" Once it was arranged, though, Joe made a demo tape of him playing and singing the first two verses of "Beige Sunshine." Graham went over to Tyrone's house the night before they went to the studio, rewinding the tape and singing along with the lyric sheet dozens of times. They were excited to be on a real punk record and get paid a cool twenty dollars each for their professional singing debut. Three years later, Direction—Graham and Tyrone's "shitty straight edge band"—opened for Glass Eye's farewell show. Fifteen years after that, Graham would be working as an Austin concert producer and promoter and get a completely insane idea of his own.

For some time, the Milkmen had prodded Beattie about reaching out to Gibby Haynes for a guest vocal. They had missed an opportunity to party with the Butthole Surfers on their *Beelzebubba* extended stay in Austin; they tried to get members of the band over to hang out at their guesthouse, but no dice.

"I don't know what killed what would have been the greatest pool party in history," said Rodney.

Gibby Haynes and Dean Clean, Austin 1990. Photo by Dan Mapp.

That year, the "Hurdy Gurdy Man" video made the Butthole Surfers icons on alternative MTV. Rodney, years away from becoming a hurdy-gurdy player himself, ran the request by Beattie again, and the stars aligned. Haynes pulled up to the studio in his new muscle car and ran inside. He was wearing his wrinkled T-shirt of Anderson Bruford

Wakeman Howe, a supergroup of disenchanted former Yes members that existed for those two years. He had no lyrics written down, but after he drew a row of penises onto some recording tape with a wax pencil, Rodney gave him a framework about a much-needed Yes reunion. After the first take, Brian stopped the tape and ran it back. It sounded kind of stupid to him.

"Can't you do that sort of . . . hollering thing?" Beattie dialed in through the God mic.

"Oh, you mean the Johnny Winter shit?" Gibby replied. "I'll do that Johnny Winter shit, then!"

They replayed the track, and Gibby nailed his second take. He walked out and invited the Dead Milkmen to come check out his cool new muscle car. They obliged, then he sped off.

Despite the level of attention MTV had afforded them in 1989, by 1990 the whole thing was starting to feel like an afterthought. Within months, Enigma would sell out to Capital Records, with Restless Records buying the Dead Milkmen back catalog from Fever to keep the CDs and tapes in stores. A pie-in-the-sky seven-album deal they'd negotiated with Enigma vaporized. By most standards, the Dead Milkmen were very successful. Their shows were selling well. More critics were starting to take them seriously. But in the contractual world, it was almost like none of it had ever happened.

In January 1991, with Operation Desert Storm the US was back at war (officially) for the first time since the Milkmen were teenagers. As the Bush I administration was deluging the airwaves to manufacture consent, Rodney led crowds in chants of "No fuckin' way / am I gonna die / in Exxon's war." The highly televised invasion was happening in a different part of the world, but as the Dead Milkmen and tour manager Dan Mapp prepared for their first tour of Europe, the world was beginning to feel a lot smaller.

Joe and David buried their hatchet enough to record a session of Ornamental Wigwam songs with Jay Schwartz producing on the sly at Overground, a company that worked with predominantly Black artists, including a Prince cover band one of the owners played in.

"The Wishniaks mixed their first record there," mentioned Schwartz. "Their engineer came in because we had some sound-processing equipment that he didn't have in his studio. It's not fully credited because it was, like, done in secret. When we did Ornamental Wigwam, the owner and his wife, [who was] this beautiful Puerto Rican woman who worked as a stripper, funded the whole operation. The owner was a pretty friendly guy, but she was all business and said, 'What are you doing?' I said, 'Well, I'm not working today, so I invited my friends in to record a couple songs.' 'Well, you've got to pay for that.'"

They moved to Adam Lasus's Studio Red, but Jay wasn't comfortable working in someone else's studio, and any hope Ornamental Wigwam had of completing an album was aborted. They recorded OW versions of two of their earliest songs—"I'm Living in Wisconsin" and "Shopper Gopper"— but they both knew their partnership was waning. Desperate for a change and some independence, Seven Morris moved up to Philly early the next year so he and Joe could write more and perhaps record Touch Me Zoo.

"I was a country kid, [and] Philly was like another level, so I was, you might say, attached to Joe like an appendage," Morris laughs. "It was quite exciting for me at the time."

With Joe preparing to leave on the first Dead Milkmen

tour of Europe, Seven moved into a bedroom in Joe's house that was vacated by the guitarist's friend Tracey, an old friend of Nina Sabatino's who would, years later, reconnect with Morris and marry him. Morris also brought a kitten, whom they named Cracker, inspired by her wafer-like color as well as the new band David Lowery formed from the ashes of Camper Van Beethoven. They nicknamed the cat "crack baby." Joe was in love, soon having anxious, silly dreams about feeding her tuna and making her throw up. All the Dead Milkmen are still, emphatically, cat guys.

Cracker the kitten, sometime in 1991. Photo by Seven Morris.

8. "ALL AROUND THE WORLD"
THE DEAD MILKMEN VS. THE ALIENS

We are not a local band, we are from outer space . . .
—"Milkmen Stomp" (1984)

One night, when he was ten, shortly after receiving his first tape recorder, Joey Genaro saw *a cigar-shaped flying ship. It landed outside on* his neighbor's pasture. Betty convinced him that it was just a vivid dream. A decade later, when he was away at college, his sister saw a similar ship, and they compared notes. Today, Joe is back living across from that vacant, quiet stretch of farmland. The only real difference is the cell phone tower adjacent to his neighbor's property that casts an eerie extraterrestrial glow on foggy nights. No matter what he and his sister really saw, and in the face of skepticism from his sci-fi-loving bandmates, *he knows about the UFOs.*

The Church of the SubGenius, whose convention the Milkmen headlined in 1985, were the most prudent pre-internet networkers of the craziest fringe groups in the world. Their pamphlets asked "Are we controlled by secret forces? Are alien space monsters bringing a startling new world?" By 1988, Rodney treated his copy of Reverend Ivan

Stang's compendium *High Weirdness by Mail* like Enigma labelmates Stryper treated their Bibles. He fired off postcards and letters to half the book, which resulted in a steady drip of variably coherent replies from conspiracy theorists avidly trying to recruit him.

"I've always been fascinated by the crazy shit that people will believe," he told *Cheap Shot Philly* in 2007. "The fact that there are millions of people running around the planet who believe *The Protocols of the Elders of Zion* are authentic speaks sadly of our species. For me, paranoid tinfoil-hat-wearing nutjobs stopped being fun once they began getting elected to public office."

Rodney Anonymous's 1990 zine. Courtesy of Seven Morris.

Rodney made a few of his own "pamphlets," including 1990's *Trekkies for Christ*, which teased theories about cheese, Frank Rizzo's secret android factory, and Gabe Kaplan, the former star of *Welcome Back, Kotter*, also known for his Groucho Marx tributes. One day, Dean was looking on when Rodney was opening stacks of mail, and one booklet he received had the title *Beyond Reincarnation: Soul Rotation!* Dean cracked up and said *Soul Rotation* would be a great album title. Rodney's collection of fringe materials had figured into some of the fence swings that composed *Metaphysical Graffiti*, including his allusion on "Epic Tales of Adventure" that "Doctors and lawyers and bankers and priests are controlled by UFOs."

With the "alternative rock" explosion bubbling, the Dead Milkmen headed into 1991 ready to record their strangest, and perhaps most nihilistic, set of songs, diving full-bore into aliens and related conspiracy theories. It wound up being their poppiest record, recorded meticulously with Fugazi's producer, and the strangest facet of all, financed by the Walt Disney Company.

"I think I'm the only person who signed the Dead Milkmen three times, and that's one of the things I might be most proud about in my life," says Wesley Hein.

In 1989, under the stewardship of Michael Eisner, Disney rebranded itself as a cradle-to-grave entity. Given the volume of plastic that *Little Mermaid* hits like "Part of Your World" and "Under the Sea" moved, Disney wanted to add a record label to their media empire. As the Disney brand was still too juvenile, and despite its address in Burbank, they gave it the broadly meaningless name Hollywood Records. The Disney brass had been courting entertainment power-lawyer Peter Paterno, who represented a stable of superstardom-bound talent that included Metallica and Dr. Dre. They asked him to be the label's president. He called up Hein, whom he heard was now a free agent after the Enigma buyout. With his brother's blessing, Wes joined forces with Paterno to become the executive vice president of Hollywood Records. They reported to work at the Walt Disney Studios on January 2, 1990, and were given offices in the animation building—a sign that Disney had no idea how labels operated.

After the Milkmen returned from their first tour of Europe in spring of 1991, things became increasingly business-like. In mid-June, Reckner, David, Dean, and Joe went up to New York City to interview prospective lawyers to negotiate their deal with Hollywood. Their lawyer, Allen Grubman, had become far too distracted by U2, whose Berlin session tapes had been stolen and widely bootlegged around Europe. Because Hollywood was the only label able to offer them what they were worth, and Reckner trusted Hein, the deal went through, with a litany of Disney clauses. One dictated that Hollywood had to approve the band's choice of producer, reserving the right to simply not release the record. Considering how *Soul Rotation* would become their "mainstream" pop record, it was a coup that they all agreed on hiring Ted Niceley. For Reckner especially, Niceley was a prize. Fugazi had finished 1990 as one of the most highly regarded rock bands in America. Though it wouldn't be until 1991 that the industry would visibly swerve, Trojan horse bands like Sonic Youth, who signed with a subsidiary of Geffen, were splintering the ceiling between the underground and mainstream.

"Some larger indies were treating bands very fucking poorly and not paying people," Ian MacKaye told Joe Gross for his book on (Niceley-produced) *In on the Kill Taker*, "and I think for a lot of bands it was like, 'Do you want to be treated like an asshole and tour in a van or be treated like an asshole and tour in a bus?'"

Like Brian Beattie, Niceley was a seasoned bassist. He also wanted to look out for guys like the Milkmen, having been through the major-label wringer himself with power-pop icon Tommy Keene. Third Story Recording's second location, where the band had done *Eat Your Paisley!*, was not up to his standards, so they moved to the Warehouse, where Philly's biggest hair-metal export Cinderella would practice. They also got to meet Billy Paul, one of the innumerable Philly soul legends most remembered (by white people, anyway) for his heartbreaking 1972 hit "Me and Mrs. Jones."

Though Joe never spoke out at the time, and he admits that Niceley and engineer Eli Janney produced a great-sounding record, he doesn't harbor fond memories of the process. The band had become accustomed to preproduction in Texas, but meetings with Niceley ran through much of July and August before Hollywood Records approved him. Joe had become used to Beattie's celebration of "magical" first takes, so Niceley's intense negotiation over changing an F chord to an F-sharp for "Shaft in Greenland" turned into an awkward standoff.

In early August, the Milkmen booked a secret gig opening for Ben Vaughn's group Pink Slip Daddy at the Khyber Pass bar in Philly. Despite (or perhaps because of) giving R.E.M. shit for playing shows under a goofy alias earlier that year, the Milkmen called themselves the "Draco Reptilians." Rodney claimed they were from Dulce, New Mexico, a remote reservation community that saw a handful of alleged, unexplained cattle mutilation cases in the seventies. Conspiracies swirled about UFOs and a legend of advanced subterranean alien facilities beneath the desert.

Only a couple *Soul Rotation* tracks would remain in Dead Milkmen sets, so the "Draco Reptilians" became a matter of curiosity among die-hard fans. In 2005, when Joe started a "bootleg of the month" feature on his website, this would be the first one he shared.

"There was practically nothing that [Rodney and I] made conversation about besides either the recording or UFOs and conspiracies the whole fucking time," said Niceley.

Rodney assumed, given how Joe was taking on more lead vocals, that he wouldn't be singing at all. He adopted the new identity of keyboardist "H. P. Hovercraft." He also obtained some cutting-edge horn stems—the same ones used by the Miami Sound Machine—and was excited to give them a whirl. However, given the ballooned Hollywood budget, Niceley sprang for the Uptown Horns, a brass quartet from New York who carved out some time. Rodney wound up singing lead on a few songs, including "How It's Gonna Be." He had built a saxophone lead on his keyboard, but he quickly brightened up when he heard how much the live quartet made his arrangement pop.

"I just *heard* horns in a couple songs," said Niceley. "Like 'Big Scary Place,' 'How It's Gonna Be,' 'Shaft in Greenland.' I was always trying to be careful of not overproducing the record, but at the same time, I was there to help them move up, move on."

Midway through November, on one of the few days the Uptown Horns were in town, Dave Blood was in bad shape. His tendonitis—a running issue for some time now—was flaring up, and flu had him sidelined for the first half of the month. Needing to move the sessions along, seasoned bassist Niceley stepped in to record scratch tracks. David was not happy about this when he returned. Niceley maintains that the mixed-down bass line on "The Secret of Life" was him. Dean suggested it may have been from a scratch track Niceley had recorded for "Shaft in Greenland," the album's closing track that also featured the Uptown Horns. There is still a question hovering about where Niceley makes an appearance.

Two tracks, "Dulce" and "Candy Coated Crime Scene," were tracked and mixed down but omitted from the CD. The former was included as filler for the "If I Had a Gun" CD single, whose cover featured a photo of Rodney's nephew, Jeff. At one point, the band had decided not to include "If I Had a Gun" on the album but recanted. Most everybody in those sessions, however, viewed "All Around the World" as a "monument," including Niceley, who remembers looking at Eli Janney in amazement while maxing out the faders, extracting every frequency from the piano chords in the ending.

"When I was comping vocals, I went for things that were really like at the top of [Joe's] range," recalls Niceley. "And I'm pretty sure Joey was working with a vocal coach at that time. I would look for things that were very . . . grasping at the note. Not that he wasn't hitting it, but it was really like up there. It just was beautiful . . . Those fucking piano chords, it's like 'A Day in the Life.' We really tried to imitate that. Eli and I just kept on turning up the faders until you can . . . hear the air conditioner or the heating ducts. It had so much of that vibe, but . . . you know, like, you come up with this album and it's really cool and then you're finding out you have to fight Nirvana and everything."

Like many veterans of the hardcore underground who were there when Black Flag released *My War*, the ubiquity of Nirvana in late 1991 was nothing special for the Milkmen.

Janney used two new hit albums, Metallica's Black Album and U2's *Achtung Baby* (a triumph of Krautrock-influenced reinvention), to incentivize the band during mix-down sessions. For every completed take, they could listen to one new song off each CD on the studio speakers.

Oddly, they applied the video budget to "The Secret of Life," the album's gorgeous and sentimental second track, which did not get released as a single. Adam Bernstein, who was now on the cusp of stardom as a video director, gathered them in Los Angeles on March 21, three weeks before *Soul Rotation* was slated for release. Bernstein visited the Unarius (an acronym for "Universal Articulate Interdimensional Understanding of Science"), an El Cajon, California-based "spiritual" organization featured in *High Weirdness by Mail*. In 1980, they had produced a "psychodrama" called *The Arrival*, which Rodney watched with his sister (it gave her the worst migraine of her life). The Unarius institute's large-scale distribution of their psychotronic videos to cable and UHF stations nationwide helped inspire the rise of post-modern live-riff programs like *Mystery Science Theater 3000*, which the Milkmen and Niceley watched on a loop during their protracted sessions.

"[Hollywood Records] gave us a bucketload of money to record *Soul Rotation*, and then did absolutely squat to promote it," Dave Blood wrote. "There was only one guy, Wesley Hein, at the company that seemed to 'get us' or even have a clue about bands that didn't have dead or dying lead singers. Naturally, the boys at Mickey's Records didn't seem to want to listen to any of his advice."

Despite his powerful-sounding position, Hein was consistently shut out of boardrooms. The band became convinced that Paterno and his army of numbers guys thought Joe was the lead singer based on the "Punk Rock Girl" and "Methodist Coloring Book" videos. The first band that Hollywood poured money into was Queen, acquiring the North American distribution rights to their back catalog for $10 million. Their music was still not available on compact disc, and according to Hein, they were out of vogue. Fueled by speculation that Freddie Mercury was HIV-positive (they had kept his illness private), the band recorded and released *Innuendo* for Hollywood in early 1991. Mercury died later that year, inspiring the rerelease of "Bohemian Rhapsody" as a single. On Valentine's Day 1992, *Wayne's World* launched the song into the stratosphere. Two months after that, while raking in profits from their Queen investment, Hollywood Records released *Soul Rotation* by the Dead Milkmen and promptly forgot about it.

Due to Hollywood's poor promotion, and cable networks' rapidly shifting priorities around music videos, "The Secret of Life" clip only aired a few times at most. Like most of *Soul Rotation*, "The Secret of Life" was not what modern rock radio sounded like by 1992, and the record's high-end production and corporate label lost them "the touch" with college radio. Many bellwethers of "the eighties" that had propelled the Dead Milkmen were being stomped out. WXPN, which had already been commandeered by what Rodney called "folk Nazis" on "The Big Sleazy," booted all its community programming in 1991, including Andy Chalfen and other *Yesterday's Now Music Today* alumni. It was a canary in the coal mine for the exponentially accelerating hacking-and-slashing of free-format stations to come that decade.

Also, as much as aliens and other high weirdness were beloved by the dorks in their hardcore audience, it wasn't something their millions of casual "Punk Rock Girl" fans leftover from 1989 understood. One year after *Soul Rotation* flopped (by Disney standards) and Hollywood Records dropped the Dead Milkmen, that changed diametrically. The Fox network green-lit a prime-time show about alien conspiracies starring two ascending sex symbols of the nineties—one of whom, David Duchovny, was Adam Bernstein's former roommate at Princeton. You couldn't make this up, but as the wheels continued to fall off the Dead Milkmen, every "brat in the frat" suddenly wanted to believe.

Acoustic in-store at Ace's Records in Tampa, Florida, November 13, 1992. Photo by Dan Mapp.

9. "I STARTED TO HATE YOU"
THE DEAD MILKMEN VS. THE DEAD MILKMEN

Identifying when the Dead Milkmen began rupturing is as much a fool's errand as pinpointing their moment of origin. Getting there, though, requires understanding a universe of external factors. Historical revisionists often mislabel either 1991 or 1994 as "the year that punk broke." The Dead Milkmen, often credited (now) with presaging the rise of "pop-punk," enjoyed few benefits of the alt-rock gold rush. It also didn't help that "selling out" was, in the heart of the nineties, a cardinal sin. By 1995, Bay Area pop-punk trio Jawbreaker signed with Geffen and then dissolved after their fans and critics terrorized them for it. In 1993, the Dead Milkmen were receiving blowback on a less sensational scale, but it was happening.

That May, under the *Newzletter* headline SELLOUT BAND GETS WHAT IT DESERVES, Joe admitted to scraping for money to do the mass-mailing. Maybe one day soon, they'd be able to mail all their subscribers electronically at negligible cost. For now, they were eagerly peddling the hundreds of leftover copies of the *Now We Are 10* CD for nine dollars, postage paid. Their back catalog had been subsumed in the Capitol buyout, so the band compiled some bootleg recordings, including their 1984 WXPN *Yesterday's Now Music Today* set, to make it publicly available for the first time. Joe printed letters from angry fans who let them know that the poppier songs on *Soul Rotation* "suck the shit off [their] ass," responding to every angry letter with a sales pitch for *Now We Are 10*.

The band had a new normal to accept. In mid-January, Joe had taken his first non-Milkmen job since 1985 at Beanie's, a UPenn coffee shop. His days were long and tiring and, from time to time, he would hear "Punk Rock Girl" on the radio and wonder how that was the same lifetime. Occasionally, Milkmen fans recognized him, wondering why he was slicing cakes and brewing coffee. Rodney found a gig as a bike courier, making *a lot of deliveries to government offices*, building the legend of Peter Bazooka. Dean, who got a job at the café in the Borders bookstore where Melissa was working, also encountered confused younger fans.

"I took a job at the Borders Books & Music in Bryn Mawr out on the snooty main line," recounts Andrew Ervin, who would later create the *Lost Tomb of the Bitchin' Chimera Dungeons & Dragons* module. "Dean was working in the café. I think he might have managed it. I had bought *Big Lizard* when it came out on a tape, so I knew who Dean was and was a bit intimidated to talk to him. And honestly, [I was] a bit surprised to see such a huge rock star working in a café. But I didn't really understand the reality at that time."

In July, Reckner and the band accepted a pitiful new contract from Hollywood that would at least get the next record out. Perhaps a fall tour with Possum Dixon, giving the band time off for the holidays, would reinvigorate them. The Milkmen did not expect much promotion. Adam Bernstein had grown quite expensive off his ass-tastic video for Sir Mix-a-Lot's "Baby Got Back," and they had no budget anyway. Within a week, the band were up in Boston, staying at Phil Sullivan's place, recording ten new tracks at Q Division with studio cofounder Jon Lupfer. Ted Niceley was overseas working on "the French *Nevermind*" with Noir Désir, and the *Newzletter* released later that summer for the next CD mentioned "no studio musicians were used for this recording."

Not Richard, but Dick—named for a prep school groundskeeper who emphatically reminded everyone how to address him—was a return to some of the band's early spitfire anger. Rodney sang lead on half the songs, shifting the equilibrium away from the band's Joe-mmercial moment. They planned to release an EP to keep the sticker price down, but Disney had no interest in pressing the album on vinyl, and filing a CD as an "EP" made no sense to them. As disappointing as the promotion behind *Soul Rotation* had been, at least Hollywood printed and shipped a respectable number of copies (in era-appropriate longboxes). They printed fewer copies of *Not Richard, but Dick*, unwittingly making it a collectors' piece decades later, when exorbitant vinyl costs made compact discs desirable to the Bastards of Young, Gen Xers, and their Zoomer kids.

"[*Not Richard, but Dick* is] the last real DM recording," commented Dave Blood years later. "'Leggo My Ego' positively smokes. We really showed how well we could play on this CD." In that opening track, Joe suggests listening to some early Brian Eno. "Baby's on Fire" sat in their cover arsenal for years before they finally decided to record it in 2025 as a B-side for their cover of Suburban Lawns' "Janitor." Other Joe-sung tracks include the Dean-penned anger anthem "Little Volcano" and "Jason's Head," a song about a two-timing woman who brutally murders her boyfriend.

"The Woman Who Was Also a Mongoose"—a nonbinary anthem that also identified as "Get Off of My Cloud"—is an understated triumph. It's a song of acceptance: both the implied acceptance of how someone chooses to identify ("If she's happy as a mongoose, it shouldn't bother me or you") and a begrudging acceptance of what was happening to the Dead Milkmen. In retrospect, it plays like the band, at their deepest subconscious and most Velvet Underground, winding things down, happily closing the door behind them, and walking away. They would come to wish that had been the case.

The song was inspired by two separate dreams. Dean had a dream where he heard a groovy Krautrock rhythm that the band worked tirelessly to re-create. Rodney, after passing out drunk on his floor one night in Center City, dreamt he was hanging out with Steve Fujita, the guitarist from Ashtray, a local band Joe had produced. In the Lynchian dream space, Rodney told Steve his new girlfriend was cool. Steve replied, "Yeah, and she's also a mongoose!"

Rodney's silly dream would come in handy. As the band jammed out Dean's new dream, Rodney started improvising lyrics. He had the words to "Get Off of My Cloud" in his memory bank, so he started riffing. They fit perfectly. The band had ragged on Elvis, the Beatles, the Doors, Led Zeppelin—why not the Stones? Dave Reckner found out there was a very good reason not to. Stealing a title like "I Am the Walrus"—which couldn't be copyrighted—as a lark was one thing, but recontextualizing lyrics was out of the question. Rodney recorded an alternate set of lyrics inspired by his mongoose dream, punctuated by playful tin whistle solos. Joe thought it was very strange but went along and recorded background harmonies. In doing so, the Dead Milkmen avoided the wrath of the Rolling Stones, who a few years later would annihilate the Verve over a brief sample used in "Bittersweet Symphony." You pick your battles, and the Milkmen were running out of fight.

Unbowed by withering label support, Reckner booked a substantial tour in two legs—one that fall and another in the winter called "Dick Is Coming." Though the internet was slowly creeping into the frame, with Dave Blood enthusiastically subscribing to CompuServe, it would still be years before Napster and iTunes cratered CD and tape sales figures. Still, corporations were already squeezing the long-reliable high-investment, higher-profit base of touring. That summer, after the Milkmen announced they were breaking up, Pearl Jam canceled their tour in a dispute over Ticketmaster's monopolization and price gouging of live venues. How far Pearl Jam moved the corporate-rock needle is still a matter of debate, but the Dead Milkmen were not active enough to participate in the conversation.

In early February, as they were practicing for leg two of the tour, the wheels fell off. Dean had never relished touring, especially since he and Melissa got married. He knew that his commercial art degree would hardly keep him competitive in "cyberspace" (as the band's beloved author William Gibson had coined the term). A favorable record deal or through-the-roof record sales may have retracted the goalposts, but the band could not make a living without touring about half the year.

"After we stopped touring (my choice really—I was tired)," Dean wrote in *Now We Are 20*, "I felt like I'd wasted ten years playing in a punk rock band. But time passes."

Dean committed to completing the "Dick Is Coming" tour and even record one more album if they could do it in Philly. He was fine with his bandmates hiring a new drummer if they wanted, unaware that Rodney was stewing and biting his tongue nearby.

"Dean and I showed up at the same meeting to quit, and he quit before I did," said Rodney that October on *Street Beat*. "It made me very irate, 'cause I wanted to be the first to quit!"

Joe and David wanted to keep the Dead Milkmen afloat, but they disagreed on how. Joe's idea was going "Beatles-after-'65 style," putting out new music and only playing in Philadelphia. This was anathema to David, who had recently parted ways with his girlfriend Jennie and did not want to be in a band that didn't tour. One week later, Rodney admitted that he was in the same boat as Dean. His bandmates had suspicions that his girlfriend Vienna and the attraction of a stable life in her native South Philly were calling him.

As much as it felt bittersweet, knowing that their last leg of "Dick Is Coming" was approaching was a relief, at least onstage. They decided not to make their impending breakup public. Though his bandmates felt a certain weight had been lifted, that weight doubled for David. His life, as he knew it, felt like it was ending, and his depression took over. As the second leg of the tour began in Kansas, the Milkmen had to be up early for a radio interview. David didn't show. Mapp called hotel management to unlock his door, and they found Dave unconscious. The memory still chokes him up.

"I got everything [needed done]," Mapp said. "We got to the hospital. They gave him the charcoal. He lived. But I felt he just needed more help before I would be comfortable."

David let his bandmates believe the painkiller overdose

was accidental, but Dan had to leave. They called Phil Sullivan in to complete the tour. After a successful gig in Boulder, where Dave's health was noticeably recovering, they rode out to San Francisco to a gig at Slim's with an East Bay pop-punk trio called Green Day. Before the show, David admitted to his bandmates what had happened in Kansas and that he had agreed to abstain from painkillers for the remainder of the run. The show also happened to be a release party for Green Day's album *Dookie*, whose artwork was strikingly similar to the *MAD* magazine aesthetic of *Beelzebubba*. Because it was their home region, the Milkmen let Green Day headline.

"I remember thinking, 'I don't wanna play after these guys—they have good songs,'" Billie Joe Armstrong later told *Rolling Stone*.

One month to the day after their show with Green Day, with *Dookie* climbing the charts, the Milkmen were back at the Trocadero, playing a raucous homecoming show to an ebullient crowd. Toward the end of their set, Dean and Dave cruised into the intro groove for "The Woman Who Was Also a Mongoose," and Rodney produced his tin whistle. Audible shrieks flew from every corner of the theater. Not to be intimidated by the Stones' mafia, Rodney and Joe busted out the lyrics to "Get Off of My Cloud" (with Joe mixing in "Mongoose" lines), but it was clear that their own bittersweet symphony had a cult. The crowd went even more crazy when Mary Linderman, in her Elsie sweatshirt, ran out from backstage and dove onto the crowd. A shaky video filmed by David's father from the balcony reveals a reluctant pride in what his son had accomplished. The band was on fire, and as Rodney said after the band closed with the Yardbirds' "Shapes of Things," surrounded by exotic dancers (one of whom he would marry later that year), "Life is good."

Time to call it.

10. "I CAN'T STAY AWAKE"
DAVE BLOOD VS. DEVOLUTION

Author's note: It would be impossible to communicate the depth and singularity of the last decade of David Schulthise's life, especially given the backdrop of Yugoslavia's devolution. Dr. Bogdan Rakić and I encourage readers to check out Peter Brock's 2005 book Media Cleansing *for more context. Let this chapter honor the memory of Dave Blood as well as all victims of US foreign policy.*

If you are considering suicide or self-harm, please remember that help is available, you don't have to go through this alone, and the world is a better place with you in it. Call or text 988 or visit 988lifeline.org.

In an interview for *Flipside* in 1994—as the Dead Milkmen were preparing to disband—Dave spoke about his looming peace with death.

"It doesn't bother me at all," he said. "The only reason being that I've gotten close to death a couple of times and it's like, 'So what?' I was real sick with asthma and it was like, 'BANG—big deal: If you die, you die.' It doesn't matter."

Interviewer: So, what are your thoughts on the afterlife? What do you think happens when you die?
Dave: You combine.
Interviewer: With what?
Dave: With whatever you are.

Dave Blood on the first Dead Milkmen European tour, 1991.
Courtesy of Dean Sabatino.

In late July 1992, a veritable army of Arizona desert cops mistook the Dead Milkmen tour van for that of a group who had fenced a warehouse full of televisions. The band got pulled over at gunpoint, with Genaro thrown in the back of a squad car, with no explanation. While being screamed at by gun-toting officers, the rest of the crew turned around one by one with their hands on their heads. David, when it was his turn, spun on one leg and danced a jig. Everyone's jaws dropped at once, but David knew this wasn't his beloved, chaotic Balkans: "What were they gonna do? Shoot us?"

Though the band had pulled back from releasing it as a single that spring, *Soul Rotation*'s "All Around the World" reflected how far the band had transcended punk as well as how far, geographically, the band had gone. In the winter of 1991, the Milkmen and Dan Mapp completed their first tour of Europe. One week after a trio of dates in Yugoslavia, that country kicked off a decade of devolution. It felt like the world was collapsing, but Dave Schulthise felt a new lease on life. He had met a nice young lady from Novi Beograd (postal code 11070), and they started exchanging letters. "All Around the World" remained his favorite Milkmen song for the rest of his life.

"Gave me goose bumps, and a weird euphoria every time we played it," he wrote in his final interview. "It took me to a place I learned about from Philip K. Dick and a girl I know who is electric-far-away."

Stanislav Žabić, who would become one of David's close friends in Belgrade, put it bluntly: "Dave felt something there in 1991."

After spending most of that February cycling around the Low Countries and Germany, they rode down to the Balkans—a powder keg of ethnic and military tensions—for gigs in Belgrade, Sarajevo, and Zagreb. Unlike other socialist countries, Yugoslavia hadn't been enveloped by the Iron Curtain, and it had long been a punk hotspot. Their promoter, Radio Zagreb veteran Ante Čikara, was forced to move their Sarajevo gig to a former bomb shelter in Banja Luka after the Boston hard-liners Slapshot had attracted skinhead violence to the original venue. The Milkmen, Mapp, and Čikara arrived as a DJ cut C+C Music Factory with Public Enemy at earsplitting volume. As the DJ transitioned to disco, Joe chatted with local teenagers about how much they hated the music and what a terrible town Banja Luka was. The Milkmen played with no opener, their set nearly ruined by fog machines and incessant flashing lights that kept throwing them off.

While David was falling in love with Serbia, his bandmates were suffering from varying levels of homesickness. Their accommodations, in a hotel that appeared to be an old lady's house, surrounded by howling wolves, did not help. In a letter to Seven Morris, Joe called Yugoslavia "one of the strangest countries we've ever been to . . . people are poorer here [than in Germany] in general. Inflation is high." Mapp still has photos of dinars that he turned into notepaper à la 1922 Papiermarks. Yugoslavia was not in the European Union, and once war became imminent, no bank in Europe would change their currency. One week after the Milkmen left Yugoslavia, war broke out and, within a few years, the country was no more.

In 1994, after their St. Patrick's Day bacchanalia, the Dead Milkmen announced a pair of farewell shows at the Trocadero early that October that would give a legion of younger fans, including Dan Stevens and Andrew Ervin, one final chance to see them play. Though they were officially "broken up," the Milkmen continued practicing in preparation, settling into their new lives around Philly. David, however, was floundering. The Milkmen had given him a ten-year gap in his résumé. Seeing Joe and Dean do so the previous year, he tried to get a service industry job at a local Boston Chicken. He lasted a day and a half before walking out, but at least they let him keep the cool hat. Soon, he had a revelation: With the war raging in the Balkans, maybe he could become part of the solution. Americans were getting a fast education in what Croatia, Bosnia, and Serbia *were*, and there was an opportunity there.

In the meantime, Reckless Records came through with a

three-album deal exacting one live album, one more studio LP, and a best-of compilation. *Chaos Rules*, cobbled together from their June 1992 and March 1994 Trocadero shows, was released in November 1994, as the heat from the finale weekend was dissipating. The contractual obligation was showing; the sound quality was mediocre, and the track list felt duct-taped together. Reckless was not allowed to include even live versions of songs on *Soul Rotation* or *Not Richard, but Dick*—something that would bite them on the *Death Rides a Pale Cow* collection in 1997 and then again when negotiating streaming rights decades later.

"Disney generally doesn't give back copyrights," said Wes Hein. "It's unfortunately just not in their DNA. . . . But then again, the label might [just not] know who this band is, because they're more focused on making Disney stars."

Even by 1994, Disney's music division was being restructured so radically that getting somebody on the phone to revert their rights for "The Secret of Life" or "If I Had a Gun" was a pipe dream. They decided to roll the dice and include a 1992 performance of the latter as an unlisted track at the end of *Chaos Rules*. It was unclear whether anybody in a position of power at Hollywood Records ever listened to it (or cared). It was hardly a blow against the empire.

That October and November—the month following their finale shows—the band dutifully tracked one last studio LP. Dean and David challenged themselves to write and sing vocals on one track apiece. Dean's loungey inclusion, "Crystalline," with music composed by David, felt like a crossover from the Mr. Shy universe. Dave Blood's industrial track, "Noise, Boys, Toys" (or "NBT"), which used a drum machine and no guitars, never made it to the mix-down stage. His greater contribution was the lyrics to

"I Can't Stay Awake," which he wrote while recovering from his hospitalization in Kansas. David harbored a glimmer of hope that the studio LP, *Stoney's Extra Stout (Pig)*, given the band's dumb luck, would somehow blow up and put them back on tour.

The naivete may have also been neuroses from moving back to Indiana at age thirty-eight to redo college. Indiana University had one of the few comprehensive programs in Serbo-Croatian culture, so David knew the road back to Serbia went through Bloomington. On New Year's Eve, his brother Kurt packed his stuff in Phil Sullivan's van ("Dave was useless in a move," Kurt laughs), and they drove to Indiana overnight. Punks all over town recognized him, wondering what a rock star was doing hanging out there and inviting him to go see the Descendents or whatever punk shows came through town. He could rarely afford to say yes. The local news station WTIU filed a feature on him, revealing his monastic lifestyle in grad-student housing, intercut with his classes with Dr. Bogdan Rakić. The two formed a close bond; both had musical backgrounds that fed into their engagement with literature, and vice versa. Rakić, born in Sarajevo in 1952, had been a classically trained clarinetist forced to "prostitute" himself and play whatever style was necessary to earn a living as a young man. He was not into punk rock, but David gave him a Milkmen shirt, which drew accolades locally.

"I would say it was given to me by a friend who was their bassist, and it was like I told them I was friends with Jesus Christ," laughs Rakić.

David entered the accelerated graduate program, taking every possible class with Rakić, who was impressed with his level of historical and political knowledge.

"David had an intellectual curiosity unique among blue-collar folks," added Bogdan. "Some people are just able to see things from a different angle. David showed me a very unique and very rare aspect of life in America, and that helped me a lot."

As soon as he'd satisfied the requirements of the Serbo-Croatian program, all he had remaining was to write a dissertation. So he quit. David had learned everything he could from Bogdan and the library; Belgrade was calling. Bogdan helped facilitate visas for him and his colleague Sarah O'Keefe. In the face of continuous conflicts and aggressive "othering" of Serbs through the Western media, they arrived in Belgrade in late 1998. Sarah's pen pal Stanislav Žabić and his family greeted them while they looked for permanent housing. David and Stanislav bonded over music and literature. Stanislav still recalls Dave's excitement upon seeing his Paul Kelly records, along with laugh-filled dinner-table stories about the Dead Milkmen. He had seen the "Punk Rock Girl" video on a bootleg VHS tape in 1990 while studying astronomy at science camp. As conflict was brewing—with his hometown Vukovar in the crosshairs—reading about American underground bands in *Rhythm* magazine had been an escape. He had even exchanged letters with Mike Watt. Now, he had the other bass-master general of American punk staying in his family's home. When David secured housing in Novi Sad and moved out, he left a copy of the *Death Rides a Pale Cow* collection CD, signed *to je musika, mog života* ("this is the music of my life").

After much negotiating of the private regional bus system (owing largely to NATO sanctions on Serbia), David resettled in Novi Sad. He found work doing English copyediting at Matica Srpska, a Serbian culture and language academy, under Dr. Svetozar Koljević, who, like Rakić, was a Sarajevan refugee. He also found work as an English tutor, something in high demand throughout eastern Europe, and he even chatted about applying his varied experiences in recording studios to help young bands get music out. David was feeling "joy and excitement" in his life for the first time in years. With help from Bishop Jovan Ćulibrk of the Serbian Orthodox Church—a former rock critic—he published historical fiction in the journal *Svetigora*. One piece was about the second generation of the Serbian dynasty, and the other was a fable about the monk who founded the Serbian Orthodox Church to reconcile his fighting brothers. David had still not reconciled his lifelong bitterness over the Catholic church, but in Serbia he had discovered what Stanislav recalls as a "new spirituality." Life was good.

Dave Blood (far right) and friends celebrate a birthday party in Belgrade, March 13, 1999 (eleven days before the NATO bombings began). Courtesy of Sarah O'Keefe and Stanislav Žabić.

In his day-to-day life, walking along the Danube River, increasingly familiar faces (of numerous ethnicities) would stop him and say how grateful they were that he was there. They loved America. Rarely did anybody mention Milošević without a profanity before or spitting on the ground after. As the winter of 1999 progressed, more reports circulated that the US and NATO were weighing an air raid, but why would they do that? David knew his government, though . . . and how they've *gotta blow up these things we don't understand.*

That March, David and his friends tried their best to maintain some semblance of normalcy as things grew increasingly terrifying. He made the challenging bus trip down to Belgrade for Stanislav's sister Snežana's birthday party. Eleven days later, NATO's bombs started raining on Serbia, including Novi Sad. On the morning of April 1, after his first steady night of sleep in weeks, David woke up to the earth shaking. He stepped outside, screaming expletives and shaking his fist at the NATO planes circling overhead. They were trying to humiliate, terrorize, and punish civilians— the people who had shown him the most love he'd ever felt in his life. His blood was boiling as he sat down to email (while he still could) friends around the country and back "home" to tell them he was getting out. Stanislav's family arranged an escape route via their apartment in Borovo Naselje, right across the Danube, where he was able to buy a flight back to New York.

Upon his return, he needed to tell as many people as he could about what he'd seen. He had kept in close contact with his ex-partner Jennie Dunham, who was working for a literary agency in Manhattan. David went straight to her home after landing in New York. MSNBC's producers were thrilled to get David on their network via satellite expecting him to add to their narrative about "evil" Serbians.

"They're bombing civilian targets, folks!" said Dave.

"You think these are civilian targets? These are still main arteries being used by Milošević . . ."

"They're bombing cigarette factories! . . . They bombed a social club, it's in a neighborhood, it's an officer's club where people drink. It's . . ."

The anchor interrupted him, refocusing on Milošević.

"Imagine if someone bombed the United States," Dave shot back. "A president with a 20 percent popularity rating would probably get a little bit of a boost up to 90 for some time. I mean, it's your country. You don't blame your leader; you blame the people bombing you."

He went into the political problems that Milošević had been having in Serbia, sliding in how foolish it was to bomb Montenegro. The anchors cut him off and abruptly went to a commercial.

Friends and family describe his return to the United States as "the end of Dave Blood." The America he was raised in no longer existed, and the US-NATO empire had robbed him of his renewed purpose. He would never learn to live with it. On April 20, as the White House and NATO dropped the single biggest payload of bombs on Serbia, two high school seniors in suburban Colorado went on a shooting rampage. The American mass-shooting epidemic was underway; songs like "Violent School" and "If I Had a Gun" suddenly had deeper and darker significance (not that he expected to ever perform them again).

David made one earnest attempt to return to eastern Europe in fall 1999, staying with Snežana in Prague for a month before it fell apart again.

"He started teaching English in Prague, working for one of the many private language schools that sprung up in eastern Europe in the nineties," she recalls, "and those schools were hungry for native English speakers, some of whom had no business teaching. That wasn't the case with Dave. He approached teaching seriously . . . I think he quit his Prague job and left for the States because he was still shocked by everything that had taken place and needed to try to truly regroup."

In 2000, Joseph Lieberman, a longtime Connecticut senator who had devoted his public life to the insurance industry, was rewarded with the opportunity to run with Al Gore in that year's election. I still remember the *Hartford Courant* deigning to call it a "miracle" on their front page. Lieberman's quest to prevent anything resembling single-payer health care in the United States had legitimized a new term that his friends in the insurance industry (and their swelling lobby) ruthlessly weaponized: "pre-existing condition." Dave Blood had been stricken with health issues for his whole life but, as he got older, it felt increasingly like America was punishing him.

The pain that made him feel like he had "too many fingers" had largely subsided after he stopped playing bass. The Milkmen got occasional pipe-dream requests to reunite. The most formidable one came in 2003 from their old friends Mickey and Aaron, who had picked up the "weirdos from rural Pennsylvania" torch in alternative rock (albeit with Butthole Surfers quantities of drugs) as Ween. Mickey (alias Dean Ween) had been a fan since he was fourteen, interviewing Joe Jack on his Trenton radio show and then the full band for his fanzine, *Yuck.* Aaron (Gene Ween), who was born in Philadelphia—nodding to it on neo-white-soul songs like "Freedom of '76"—gave the Dead Milkmen an avid shout-out on MTV during the waning years of video programming. Both bands had been given the "What the hell is this crap?" treatment by *Beavis and Butt-Head*. Still, the Milkmen did not want to play without Dave Blood, and Joe already had a summer tour booked with his band the Low Budgets.

The Milkmen did "reunite" one last time that year to record commentary for the *Philadelphia in Love* DVD collection and take photos for the accompanying *Now We Are 20* reissue of the *Now We Are 10* recordings. In a moment of quintessential rock 'n' roll weirdness, they fielded a request from Corey Feldman to record a cover of "I'm Flying Away" for *Jumpin' Jesús on a Pogo Stick*, a tribute compilation on longtime fan Andrew Bentley's Crazy Bastard Records. As the profit margin on CDs was crashing that year, the tribute compilation never came out, but Feldman included it on his solo album *Former Child Actor*. Bentley paid $160 for the rights to print it on two thousand copies of the CD, many of which still sit in his garage.

Watching the US invade and occupy yet another country in Iraq that April, David's health further deteriorated, and he was barely eating. Margie got diagnosed with cancer, and the added weight of her health problems compounded the stresses between her husband and her son. As September 16—David's forty-seventh birthday—approached, he decided it would be his last. While his family gathered around the cake, he retreated with a cocktail of pills. Kurt walked in and found his brother babbling and out of sorts. As fast as their father had driven him from his high school graduation party, his brother sped him to urgent care. David spent two weeks recovering in a mental health facility; his former bandmates came to check in.

David's brothers made the decision to separate him from his father. Up in Westchester County, New York, Jennie and her husband, Craig, had a new house and were preparing to welcome their first child. David could stay with them, perhaps helping out with childcare, while he got back on his feet. David found their domestic situation remarkable.

"You're not fighting. You're not yelling at each other!" he remarked one day.

"No," Jennie said, laughing it off.

"You just love each other," said David.

"Yep," said Jennie, going about her day, taking notice how unaccustomed David was to such a peaceful home.

By late 2003, David started feeling a future again. In the teeth of America's war on its own sick, they offered to "hire" David as a live-in nanny, endowing him with health care. Increasingly embittered about America under Bush II, he turned his attention back to the former Yugoslavia, where he read that much of the diplomatic smoke was beginning to clear. He knew he needed to be in Serbia to continue his life, teaching and learning again.

In January 2004, Margie declined rapidly. None of her treatments were working, and she realized that she needed to come home to enter hospice. David got the call at Jennie's, and they got in the car to drive down to Ridley Park. They pulled in that evening, arriving in the waning moments of Margie's lucidity. Jennie placed her baby in Margie's arms to introduce them. By the next morning, David's mother was no longer speaking. Jennie and Craig brought their baby home to Westchester; David stayed behind to be there for his mother's final days. He secretly pocketed her end-of-life drugs.

The following month, David opened his email and saw Stanislav's name. His grandmother, who'd anchored them through a traumatic decade, had passed away. They got on the phone and talked for hours about how strong she had been and how much they missed her, as well as their lives in Serbia that had been stolen from them. By then, Stanislav had resettled in Cleveland and Snežana in Chicago; David never felt like he could truly resettle in the United States. They made noncommittal plans to see one another.

By early March, David weighed less than one hundred pounds. He cared for baby Edward while Jennie was at work in the city, but he took less care of himself. On the night of March 8, he left a comment on Dean's blog, sharing an old memory of Rodney telling a joke about jacking off on a Cleveland radio show. He sent his old friend Bogdan an email, expressing concern about the ongoing elections in Serbia. The following day, Jennie, Craig, and their baby son left town overnight. David called her, sad and anxious about being alone in the large house in the country. She assured him that they'd be back the next day.

When they got home the following evening, they put Edward to bed and then chatted and laughed at the table. David had a smile and look of relief on his face. Everything seemed okay. Remembering that tomorrow was a typical workday, they all turned in. David Schulthise went upstairs to his room, turned the light on, catching a glance at his nightstand. Next to his Saint Sava icon stood his favorite picture: him standing there in his blue pj's, embracing baby Edward with a classic, goofy "Dave Blood" expression on his face. His note nearby thanked Jennie for all the love and peace he had found in her home that he hadn't known elsewhere. He wished for his savings to go to the Studenica

Monastery, which he knew would help the Serbian people. With the light still on, he swallowed his mother's pills, lay down, and combined.

That November, the Dead Milkmen reunited, along with F.O.D., Electric Love Muffin, and other compatriots for two concerts at the Trocadero to honor Dave Blood. Jennie made magnets as gifts for donors to the Studenica Monastery featuring a picture of an ebullient Dave onstage in a Girl Scout uniform all those years ago (which Dean displayed on his kick drum). On March 27, 2006, two years to the day after David's memorial service, Jennie welcomed her second son. They named him Ridley.

Donor magnets from the 2004 Dave Blood memorial concerts.
Courtesy of Jennie Dunham.

"Every now and then I've caught myself [thinking], 'I shouldn't be having fun, this is a memorial show,'" Rodney told *City Paper* as the shows approached. "But then I think—what used to crack Dave up was when we first started playing, punk bands never smiled. And they didn't have fun onstage. He played the hell out of that thing, and he smiled every minute. . . . It was never a thought in our heads of ever replacing anyone. I've always said we were like this great example of a utopian commune. We shared all writing credits and all money. And we would have waited forever for him."

11. "MEANINGLESS UPBEAT HAPPY SONG" THE DEAD MILKMEN VS. THE INTERNET

Two-three-four . . .

The Dead Milkmen broke up at a perfect time for Web 2.0 (the read/write web) like America Online to expand onto the family computers of their new generation of fans, many of whom never got to see the band live. Dan Stevens, who did finagle his way into the final-final show in 1994, used one of his first web searches ever to look up the Dead Milkmen. Just in time for the band to stop touring, Dean launched DeadMilkmen.com, and its attendant message boards (d)evolved into the DM Free-for-All, a vibrant fan community in an optimistic moment for the internet toward the new millennium.

In October 1995, when Reckless finally released *Stoney's*, it landed with a resounding yet understandable thud. The *Vancouver Sun* said there were two good things about the record: the mid-tempo ska shuffle "I'm Flying Away," and that it was the final Dead Milkmen album. Jonathan Takiff of the *Philadelphia Daily News* loved it: "Maybe this album will sell a million copies and force the band to reunite. We can wish." Joe and David also privately held on to this naive belief as they were tracking it—a delusion that faded over 1995.

"I cannot remember reading a review or even a description," said Joe years later. "We received a lot of positive mail about it, but also a lot of mail saying please don't break up and come back on tour. It was kind of bittersweet."

Joe was distraught, sending a bunch of his Milkmen paraphernalia out to pen pals. He'd confided in David that he was not happy with the progress of Touch Me Zoo, largely owing to squabbles about the direction of the band. As much as the MTV experience helped him realize he lacked "rock star" programming, it was rough going from a sold-out Trocadero to DIY gigs at nearly twice the age of some of the performers and bookers.

Woods and Dan Stevens, in bucket hat and Elsie shirt, respectively, watching Touch Me Zoo. Brian Sprenger on drums with Joe Genaro visible over his right shoulder. Yardley Masonic Temple, November 25, 1995. Photo by Chris Siegel, courtesy of Dandrew Stevens.

One such show took place at the Yardley Masonic Temple roughly a month after *Stoney's* hit shelves, and one such scene kid half Joe's age was Dan Stevens. The headliners, Plow, were not yet United, and Stevens was not yet Dandrew. When it came time for Touch Me Zoo's set, he camped out up front. He'd exchanged a couple of letters with Joe but spent the whole set working up the nerve to introduce himself in person.

Shortly after Joe returned from grabbing food, TMZ drummer Brian Sprenger introduced him as "Andy." Dan quickly corrected him as Plow United set up and plugged in, blanketing the space with noise. A few minutes later, Dan worked up the courage to go over and reengage Joe. He said he loved *Stoney's Extra Stout (Pig)*, a compliment for which Joe was wholly unprepared. As Plow United got louder, Joe turned back to Dan.

"WHAT'D YOU SAY YOUR NAME WAS? ANDREW?" Joe asked.

"NO, IT'S DAN!!"

"DAN-DREW??" Joe joked.

That exchange was similar to one embedded in punk history. In 1981, Sue McLane (alias Su Tissue) met a friend at a loud party and asked what he did for a living. He replied, "I'm a janitor," and she misheard, "Oh, my genitals." This exchange became the chorus in the Suburban Lawns' "Janitor." If you had told Stevens, in that moment, that exactly three decades later he and Joe Jack Talcum would be recording a Dead Milkmen cover of "Janitor"—to post on the *internet*—he would have likely shit his pants. Regardless, with Plow (soon United) shaking the walls of the Yardley Masonic Temple, Dan Stevens, dorky bassist of Farquar Muckenfuss was a memory. *Dandrew* was born.

"I had already been writing [Joe] letters back and forth a little bit at that point, and then the next, signed it 'Dandrew.' And it just kind of stuck," he said. "I've had bosses at totally non-music-related jobs calling me Dandrew."

Working on his degree at Temple, Stevens scraped

together his rent with a variety of jobs in sectors the internet was fast depleting, including a Blockbuster Video on the corner of Second and South. Dan and his roommate convinced their manager, a gruff *fuckin' Philly* guy (who moonlighted as a flashy Mummer and got them high before every shift) to diversify their catalog with foreign art films and indie hits like *Kids*. The job wore thin by early 2001, when a congregation of the worst people in Philly decided to celebrate Mardi Gras by starting a five-alarm riot.

By then, Dandrew was playing with Joe in a new band called the Low Budgets. In 2000, Chris Seegel broke up the Town Managers—his trio with Genaro (whom he had named Jonk Provoc)—to start a new band. He invited Joe to play organ as they started "valuerock"—a zippy and economical play on the Minutemen's "jamming econo." Chris recruited Dandrew, whom he knew from Temple, to play bass. Dandrew had taught himself to play bass along with *Big Lizard* and was ecstatic playing in a band with one of his heroes. In 2002, Joe introduced Dandrew to Kurt, whom he told flat out to "tell your brother Dave that he's the best bass player in the world!"

The next time Dandrew saw Kurt, he ran up to him. "Well?"

"I told Dave that, and he said you're crazy!" replied Kurt.

Kurt and Joe Schulthise had been spending the previous couple of years trying to get David out of Ridley Park with little luck. Dandrew had no idea about the extent of what his favorite bassist was going through; he was just happy Dave Blood knew he existed.

In 2004, though everyone was still reeling from David's

death, Joe began to enjoy touring again in his forties. Joe's company issued him a "massive brick" that enabled his laptop to access Wi-Fi, a novelty at the time. In 2005, a columnist for PitchforkMedia.com (later *Pitchfork*, later Condé Nast, always on Rodney's shit list) quoted Joe in a piece about how the internet had facilitated "soft selling out" and enabled musicians to work while touring. It is the only extant mention of the Dead Milkmen in that site's history. The Dead Milkmen had purposefully never elevated themselves above Best Western quality on the road, so once Joe could afford a reasonable room for the Low Budgets, he was happy to provide. He didn't mind that his younger bandmates showed up plastered; nobody had to sleep on a stranger's floor, deal with bedbug infestations, or wake up with a gun in their face.

"Three of the four Low Budgets were taking off six weeks at a time [from a production house]," said Stevens. "We didn't destroy a hotel room, but we made forts out of cushions and stuff when we were tripping and drinking. And Joe was out in the business lounge working while we were being animals."

One day before a spring 2004 show in West Philly, the unthinkable happened.

"It was before the drinking started," Steven recalls, "and Joe in his own 'Joe' way was like, 'So, we're gonna do a memorial show for Dave. Would you like to play bass?'"

Dan was shaking. He didn't know what to say. He said he didn't know.

"I immediately [thought] nobody can replace Dave Blood . . . It felt really kind of daunting."

And then he got drunk.

"We played the show, and it was normal chaos. I probably

broke the bass amp or something. Afterwards, I was like, 'Joe, I'll totally fucking do it because I know every one of those fucking songs!'"

With six months to go before the memorial shows, Dean, Rodney, and Joe started getting together with Stevens to practice. It was premised as an "audition" for Dandrew, but the 1983 "audition" that solidified the Dead Milkmen wore quotation marks too.

"I found out I was the only one that auditioned," he admits. "It went really well—all I had to do was ask Joe which key a [song] was in."

As November approached, the band told *City Paper*, emphatically, that this was just a party to honor Dave Blood. It was not a reunion. Given the somber and celebratory duality of the memorial shows, Dan kept his head down and nailed the job. During the intro to "Bitchin' Camaro," Rodney—who had never met Dandrew before their first rehearsal—called him out for a big round of applause, thanking "this guy" for helping them out. After the applause died down, he commented that maybe, one day, he would learn his name. Dan's sister made him a scrapbook: "When Dan was a Dead Milkman."

"We all thought this was just a two-off thing as a tribute for Dave," he notes, "and I was happy with that. I didn't think we were gonna do anything, and we didn't for four more years."

In the interim, as Joe began an unplanned career as a troubadour, things continued to feel scary and hollow. In 2005, Ram Ayala from Taco Land was murdered over the pittance in his cashbox in a rash of armed robberies plaguing San Antonio. In 2006, Rodney took special notice of a striking civil liberties case in Georgia, where Homeland Security had poured surveillance resources into tracking and arresting an animal rights protestor named Caitlin Childs. Her "offense" was photographing the vehicle of someone who had photographed her protest at the Honey Baked Ham facility outside Atlanta. Apparently, American national security rested upon honey baked ham. Five and three years into the illegal occupations of Afghanistan and Iraq, respectively, it felt like the war was coming home, and everything seemed bleak. It became clear how right Dave Blood had been.

On a bad depression day, Rodney wound up at Electric Ferret records, where the clerk Patrick Rogers recommended a CD on his label by the Aussie electro-industrial group Angelspit. Hearing it folded his depression into anger that the whole world was forced to listen to "faux-hemian" oatmeal like Norah Jones. More people needed to hear noise, especially considering how most people's knowledge of industrial—the new punk rock—ended with Nine Inch Nails.

"I have no problem with people being familiar with Chvrches, but when everybody's heard of them and very few people have heard of Ambassador21, the system is obviously broken and needs to be fixed right the fuck now," Rodney told an interviewer.

He taught himself to DJ and started an internet radio show to accompany his blog "Rodney Anonymous Tells You How to Live." He still programs a monthly show from his home in South Philly, promoting newer and overlooked works by dark, electronic artists—the more destructive to gender norms and polite society, the better. He routinely hits friends and followers over the head with artists like

Plack Blague (America's Leather Band™), the Genitorturers (authors of the inimitable "Cum Junkie," as cited on *Quaker City Quiet Pills*), and dark underground artists like Lana Del Rabies (alias Sam An).

"[Rodney] apparently praised me in front of a crowd at their Phoenix show on tour [in 2019], who generally didn't really know who I was," said An, who had moved to LA for wider opportunities in art and music. "When I was younger, I recall [my dad] talking about going to a Dead Milkmen show when he was in his twenties with his best friend at the time. So, needless to say, my dad was impressed."

Graham Williams had a mission. South by Southwest had become the biggest music festival in America, and his Fun Fun Fun Fest provided a counterpoint for those who kept Austin weird. In early 2008, they were preparing for their third year, having grown from roughly eight thousand people to an expected twenty thousand. He had a list of "wouldn't it be crazy if . . ." bands, and the Dead Milkmen were on the top. Other than his lifelong fandom, it was a wise business decision.

"They checked a lot of boxes," said Williams. "They were appreciated by the skater, hardcore types; they were appreciated by the college-rock R.E.M. crowd; the acid-trippy Butthole Surfers crowd; anything left of center."

He decided to visit Brian Beattie for a favor, reminiscing about him and Tyrone going to Arlyn to record "Beige Sunshine" as excited kids. Now an excited adult, the process grew into a full-court press involving various old friends and well-wishers around Austin. None of the Milkmen flat-out refused, but there was a merry-go-round of nobody wanting to break the ice. They still had a soft spot for Austin, but they hadn't played there in fifteen years when they busked outside Compact Disc Austin before their final Liberty Lunch gig. After the consortium sweetened the deal with $20,000, Joe, Rodney, and Dean laid down their arms. What reason did they have to leave that offer on the table? Plus, Dandrew was still on board, and where the weeds of minutiae needed conquering, Reckner and Mapp were still there with machetes.

"It was very validating after a really dark, kind of long, melancholy [period]," said Reckner. "There were several thousand people out there that just thought it was the greatest . . . My kids were onstage [while the Milkmen] were playing all the stuff they had heard about, and what 'Dad used to do.' It was just really emotionally lifting: they're playing and people are screaming with the lyrics . . . it was not like a throwback show, it was something completely different."

One of the biggest crowds the Milkmen ever played for spread out in front of them, filled with multiple generations of fans who never thought they were going to see this. In 1990, Rodney would yell "Touch my keyboard and die!" In 2008, he was crowd-surfing with it. Any apprehension Dean, Joe, and Rodney felt melted away once they started practicing with Dandrew again, but now they were co-headlining a festival with Bad Brains, All, and Clipse. They could also say hi to their old friends in Killdozer.

Later that night, the ever-industrious Joe had a solo gig at Beerland. Still buzzing from the festival set, Dandrew and Rodney rewarded themselves with an irresponsible number of beers. The two chatted and looked on as Joe began his set. Suddenly, Rodney took a swig, turned to Dandrew, and said, "I can't wait to record some new stuff!" and walked away.

"I was like, 'Holy shit, this is happening,'" recalls Stevens.

On January 2, 2009, Dean, Joe, and Rodney met with Dave Reckner. Rodney wanted the Dead Milkmen to start playing again. Joe and Dean were amenable to the idea, but they needed to address some elephants in the room. Rodney had no interest in being in a paunchy legacy band, churning out their "greatest hits" at county fairs or, even worse, bending over for the rising anti-futurism of playing "classic albums, front to back." They were going to practice frequently. They were going to write and record new music, and enjoy themselves in the process, or it wasn't happening. Dean still had no interest in touring, especially now with his son Victor in grade school, but he was willing to entertain weekenders. Get on a plane in Philly, land somewhere, go make a bunch of people happy, and go home. They would hire Dandrew as a contractor, paying him to practice and play gigs, but they weren't comfortable with making him a member of their LLC unless they knew things were going to stick.

Thanks to advances in home-recording software and the attendant rise of affordability (or piracy, where applicable), all four of the Milkmen had digital audio workstations. In 1994, the idea of being able to email or file-transfer a demo was like walking on Mars. Fifteen years later, they could attach an MP3 while sitting on the toilet. One of Dandrew's favorite incomplete pieces was a jumpy demo he'd made for Farquar Muckenfuss years prior, specifically trying to sound like a Dead Milkmen song.

"I did a newer demo of it, and within twenty-four hours, Rodney sent an email back, and he wrote almost exactly what's on the record for lyrics over it."

They dubbed it the "Meaningless Upbeat Happy Song." It harkened back to crowd favorites "Stuart" and "I Dream of Jesus," albeit from a point of view more aligned with Rodney's own, reminding people if they weren't depressed, they should be. As 2009 moved along, their collective pent-up itch spilled into a set of new demos that led them to Miner Street Recordings with Brian McTear and Amy Morrissey.

"Rodney was really diving deep into reinvention in that time off," said McTear. "He was actually the only person I knew at the time who would refer to all his sounds as 'VSTs' [Virtual Studio Technology plug-ins]. He was just 'VST this, VST that.' I knew that the digital sounds in a computer were called VSTs, but I never really heard people so affectionately refer to them as that. I remember in Burn Witch Burn, he started playing his hurdy-gurdy and weird shit like that, so it made sense that when they came back, he wanted to be not just singing but also playing."

The result, a seventeen-track album Dean sold off their website called *The King in Yellow*, played like an old friend returning after wandering the globe for years, dying to share their slideshow. Rodney adapted a catchy demo of Dean's into a tribute to Caitlin Childs. Eighteen years after their ballooned Disney budget let the Uptown Horns wash out his Miami Sound Machine stems, he added an artificial horn section to Joe's manic triumph, "Can't Relax."

"Everybody should quit for ten years," said Rodney. "Seriously. Stop it! Stop it now! If you're just turning out crap, stop it! Take a break, go do something else. Then come back."

In a moment of unfettered liberal optimism, their cynicism could not have been more needed. The Dead Milkmen were back.

After some pressure, they printed a limited run of compact discs for those who still demanded plastic. CD players were already being removed systematically from new computers, and within a few years they would disappear from new cars as well. The Milkmen—Rodney especially—were incredulous that the "vinyl revival" snuck up on them. Now that they were active again, generations of fans took to social media—something the band adopted begrudgingly—asking about vinyl reissues. Rodney would reply that he didn't have a turntable, nor did he "own a butter churn."

The rest of the band were okay with pressing their new singles on (pointedly) limited runs that would certainly sell out and turn a neat little profit they could reinvest in recording time. They pressed and shipped through a third-party vendor, who made them choose a shell name for their "label"; Rodney called it "Quid Ergo," which translated (loosely) to "whatever." Sustainability, as they had laid out at their January 2, 2009, meeting, would need to be a pillar of their new business model. Planning to record and promote new music felt like being a divorcée plunging back into the dating world after fifteen years of marriage, suddenly needing to optimize their attractiveness on OkCupid and navigate obnoxious new brain-rot trends. Having Graham Williams in their corner after the Fun Fun Fun reunion was crucial.

"Dave Reckner hit me up about San Francisco," said Williams. "He mentioned how they looked up whatever midsize clubs still existed [from the nineties] and was running into issues with younger promoters."

One booker, weaned during the digital era, asked them to send over their SoundScan data for consideration. Reckner responded that they had not been an active band in over fifteen years and had none of those numbers to share. The promoter paused and grappled for an alternate route that would satisfy their bosses.

"So, who did you play with the last time you were in San Francisco?"

"Um [clears throat] . . . Green Day."

Two great disruptions to popular culture both crept up toward the end of the Dead Milkmen's hiatus: user-generated streaming video, and the smartphone. YouTube went online in the spring of 2005, quickly cornering the emerging market of video-sharing on the internet. That first year, the first video that surfaced in a search for "dead milkmen" was a found-footage-style "documentary" that featured a group of suburban burnouts driving and singing along to "V.F.W." before getting drunk and mooning the camcorder. It's a distant memory now, but even if the whole thing was staged, it lived every impulse of that song. *Maybe it's cause of the way [they] look, or maybe it's something else.*

In October 2006, Google purchased YouTube, transforming the upstart streaming site into a minefield of potential litigation by music rights holders, now with disgusting amounts of capital. A new generation of nerdcore rappers, who grew up listening to the Dead Milkmen drop references to obscure TV actors and doomsday cults, built audiences online. One of the most successful was a

Bay Area fan named Andrew Nielsen, who, as MC Lars, accrued millions of views and a global fanbase via MySpace, Facebook, and YouTube.

"I was on the Warped Tour in 2011, and I did some really long interview, and someone asked me my goal as an artist," said Lars, "and I said I always wanted to, like, be someone who's respected in the indie scene who never sold out, right? Like the Dead Milkmen. I said they're like my barometer of what success means."

Soon after the interview made its rounds, Lars received a gracious email from Rodney Anonymous. They hit it off with granular conversations about Edgar Allan Poe— Rodney was particularly salty that Baltimore, not Philly, got his body—which resulted in the Dead Milkmen guesting on a rewritten version of Lars's 2012 single "Mr. Raven." At their Halloween show that year, Rodney and Dean took Lars over to the historic house.

"There was a raven statue, and I was dressed in my Poe costume," recalls Lars. "I tried to climb over the fence to take a picture with it. Dean and Rodney both ran away, 'cause they're like, 'Lars, this is a federal monument. You're gonna get arrested. And most of the people in federal prison aren't there for taking pictures at the Poe house.'"

As Google jaws-of-life'd YouTube onto every smartphone on the planet, it had the desired impact on Dandrew's adolescent sons, Edgar and Junius. Edgar mentioned that his dad's band needed to beef up their presence; there were plenty of shaky live videos of his dad playing bass, but not much curated by the band themselves.

In late January 2020, the Milkmen met up for practice. Completely unaware of what was coming that March, and Joe with a late-winter solo tour booked, the four agreed to take the year off from shows to focus on completing their new album. In 2017, they'd collaborated with the Philly charity label the Giving Groove to release the six-song EP *Welcome to the End of the World*. Now, they were halfway to a full new LP, with ten songs ready and three in the can.

"So, anyone have any other ideas?" Rodney asked before their meeting adjourned.

"Um," Dan spoke after a few pregnant seconds, "Edgar said we should do something about our YouTube presence."

Rodney's eyes lit up.

It's fun to speculate what may have happened to the fictional Dead Milkmen had the real iteration never materialized. Had Joe chosen to go to Boston University to study TV production, would "the Dead Milkmen" have resurfaced as a *Monkees*-style sitcom? Would they have pulled an elaborate heist of the Liberty Bell and dumped it into the Delaware? Would they have recorded a "haunted" album in the basement of the Edgar Allan Poe house (as Rodney later *did*, albeit with permission)? Would it have "jumped the shark" like many of their favorite TV shows?

As it happened, Dan Mapp went on to road-manage the Monkees' reunion and nostalgia tours, and the Milkmen were never more starstruck than when he introduced them to Mickey Dolenz and Mike Nesmith. Rodney had cited the Monkees as the "greatest punk rock group in the world." In 1994, Marge Simpson's psychotherapist reinforced that the Monkees "weren't about music . . . They were about rebellion, about political and social upheaval!"

The real Dead Milkmen had much in common with the Monkees, other than the obvious being four divergent personalities perpetually struggling against "the man/ industry." Though Rodney wasn't on the lease, like the Monkees, the Milkmen all lived in the same house in West Philly between their first two albums and tours. In 1968, the FBI built a file on the Monkees over their film *Head* (for which Dolenz sued in 2022). In 1990, the Secret Service came to RAW Ltd. to shake Rodney down just because he allegedly wrote "kill the president" above an autograph in Utah.

The week after Dandrew delivered his son's comment about YouTube, Rodney arrived at practice with a video camera, eagerly grilling his bandmates as they set up. Dean contributed a beep-and-boop retro-newsroom jingle to *Big Questions with the Dead Milkmen*. The "show" employed minimal editing and featured ungodly headroom ratios. Despite having bandmates with degrees in commercial art and Radio-TV-Film (and two having Gen-Z sons), Rodney's production felt purposeful in its rawness.

In early March, as the pandemic crept in, the format changed, extending the lifespan of *Big Questions* by several years. Though Rodney still had a heavy hand in the new Zoom variant of the series, all four appeared in one quarter of the screen, often scrambled so the order changed every week. As a sanity-retention measure, they traded off the big question. Three guys who grew up watching *The Monkees* (and one who grew up on Monkees-inspired Saturday-morning cartoons) suddenly had their own show. In *Newzletter 34.5* in 1986, Joe wrote of a dream he had about *The Adventures of the Dead Milkmen*, a Saturday-morning cartoon about four Milkmen who get killed, returning as ghosts with superpowers. *Big Questions* may not have had a TV-network budget, but they did incorporate silly animations and practical effects, go on adventures (filming their sojourns out to punk festivals), and regularly make each other lose their shit. Best of all, as DAWs had done a decade prior, web-conferencing made it possible for them to produce it weekly from the comfort of their own homes.

"I can't tell you how many people have said either in comments on the videos or to me in person, 'I love *Big Questions*—it's like my Saturday-morning cartoons!'" said Dandrew. "We would always post them on early Saturday mornings. We would have at least one thousand [views, which is] like selling out a show in, like, a midsize club."

In a sea of forced subsumption to the internet for much of 2020, the show felt like getting a new spoken-word Dead Milkmen track every weekend. They still collaborated on demos, and when inspiration struck, the results were uploaded and the audio recordings were filed onto a new splinter Bandcamp page as the quasi-official album *"Depends on the Horse . . ."* In 2025, "Fred Lettuce" resurfaced on YouTube (sounding an awful lot like Rodney) as a discombobulated old man telling people how to purchase the new Dead Milkmen single, "When Daddy Drinks." Long live Lettuce.

"I had that realization that even though nobody's playing gigs, we're still putting content out there that has to do with the band," Stevens added. "It was a cool feeling just keeping something going, because who knows if we hadn't done that, we probably wouldn't have put out *Quaker City Quiet Pills.*"

To many fans, the YouTube show acted as a revival of the website's millennial Free-for-All, with comment sections turning into fields for viewer questions, anecdotes, and inevitably, a platform for the shrinking sliver of older fans with terrible opinions about science and politics.

"If you think that racism or sexism have a place in punk rock, we are not the band for you, nor have we ever been the band for you," Rodney stated clearly in one early episode.

The show provided a forum for a healthy exchange of ideas that, like their music had for decades, demonstrated that it was still possible to see the world in different ways yet remain united in purpose. It also tracked how the COVID era affected the Milkmen individually. Joe, in a new relationship with his boyfriend Jason, had to leave Conshohocken to return home to Coatesville to care for his elderly parents, parting ways with Andy Chalfen and Dean's instrumental band I Think Like Midnight. Dan's marriage ended, placing him in a series of literally and symbolically inconsistent places as he assumed custody of his three sons and an erratic work schedule.

When they decided to move on to other projects, including a Bandcamp-only singles series for 2025, the Milkmen had produced over two hundred episodes of *Big Questions*, far outpacing the Monkees' sixty-eight (plus the related spin-off movies). Additionally, the "mainstream media" further disintegrated, leaving a handful of exceptionally ignorant white dudes on the internet with an ahistorical level of influence. A rare saving grace during the lockdown and the subsequent age of accelerated unreason was: If you're going to listen to four white dudes talking to each other on the internet, it may as well be the Dead Milkmen.

12. "WELCOME TO THE END OF THE WORLD" THE DEAD MILKMEN VS. NOSTALGIA

"The Dead Milkmen are people who had one existence in the era of major labels, and reformed after that era was long gone . . . and decided how they were gonna go about just doing this for the rest of their lives," said Brian McTear in 2015 as the band set up nearby. "You get the sense that they're having a lot of fun."

Rodney, Dean, Dandrew, and Joe surround their friends Sheila Sullivan and Stewart Frescas, Chicago, 2015. Courtesy of Sheila Sullivan.

Increasingly, that fun is an act of resistance and pillar of sustainability for the Dead Milkmen as the 2020s trudge along and everything that held the band down in their so-called heyday—the music industry and capitalism—are going down in flames and shooting everything that moves. Admittedly, it's insane that a band with songs about puking, drinking bleach, and wrecking buses full of mentally handicapped people would remain so relevant, almost despite their best efforts.

"Society keeps getting some things right—like the legalization of same-sex marriage—and it keeps making some huge mistakes," Rodney told *PennLive* in 2014. "Until society can get its act together, we'll have to keep writing songs."

This is also why they have no use for nostalgia: Everything that pissed them off four decades ago is still out there in some form, with the smart parts getting smarter and the dumb parts getting cartoonishly dumber. When the band formed and recorded their first few albums, the president was a brain-dead celebrity with an "onald" name who race-baited his way into politics, lied pathologically, tried to legislate queer people out of existence, unilaterally defunded public services, supported mass-incarceration programs at home and mass-extermination programs abroad, empowered white supremacists while perpetuating a myth of "white victimhood," and invaded several countries for no good reason. Dave Blood once wrote that "economics is called 'the dismal science' for good reason—nothing good has come of it so far. Economics is often used as an excuse for exploiting the average Joe. . . . You hear nonsense/double-talk like this tossed out in the press by so-called leading economists." In other words, anybody who was dumb enough to believe "trickle-down economics" in 1985 was dumb enough to believe anything in 2025.

The conspiratorial world the Dead Milkmen outlined

forty years ago seems utopian today. In 1988, the "Bleach Boys" hung out and chug(a-lug)ged bleach in a scenario as far-fetched as the Angry Samoans imploring listeners to poke their eyes out in "Lights Out." Thirty-two years later, in the face of a pandemic, the "Leader of the Free World" gave air to the idea that bleach may be a preventative measure. The insurgent virality of "Bleach Boys," given streaming revenues in 2020, may have netted the Dead Milkmen a cool ten dollars. Similarly, a country where functional adults genuinely believed that Hillary Clinton ran a child-sex ring in a nonexistent basement makes an augmented reality where a wacko raving about landing strips for gay Martians in the Des Moines hinterland seem reasonable. In 2025, driven by a deep-web conspiracy about "white genocide," the American oligarchy granted Afrikaners refugee status, resettling some in a Midwestern city whose white majority had slipped precipitously: Des Moines, Iowa. But I'm sure that's just a coincidence, Stuart. *Beelzebubba* had not suddenly become a field guide to a rotting empire—it has always been one.

The only meaningful difference forty years later is that boredom and imagination—those most human of phenomena that made the Dead Milkmen possible—have been colonized by smart phones and algorithms. The very act of buying a record, CD, or tape and giving it your undivided attention has become a political act. So has the steadfast refusal of the Dead Milkmen to stop creating. They've long been a "hand-me-down" band for Gen-X fans and their Gen-Z kids, but the glowing radical empathy practiced by their younger fan base makes perfect sense.

"I always felt like the things Rodney said resonated with my own thoughts and cynicism of the world, like he was speaking my own thoughts out loud," said bassist Brooke Feenie of queer Philly punk trio Froggy. "They never take themselves too seriously, which I think is so important when you are young and a huge part of finding your identity."

Feenie credits the "silly, carefree nature of the Dead Milkmen" with inspiring much of Froggy's early music, especially "7-Eleven Nachos," which drew a serious partnership with the convenience store chain (who sponsored their music video) and a placement on the *Clerks III* soundtrack. In 2024, they held a five-year anniversary party for their band, and put together a hardcore show with F.O.D.

To move further down the list of bands just in the Philly area who owe a debt of gratitude to the Milkmen would fill another book. One working theory I've long held is that every artist in Philadelphia has at least one Dead Milkmen story. I tested this theory when filmmaker Jason Taylor screened his 2024 movie *Cast & Crew* at the Central Michigan International Film Festival. He was cursed by a late slot that closed out the weekend. I had been managing the Broadway Theatre that evening and snuck into the house for the Q&A. Taylor answered a boilerplate question from one of the organizers, then that nervous moment came when both started looking around the thin audience. I raised my hand and asked if he had any Dead Milkmen stories. Taylor's expression visibly brightened. He smiled, chuckled, and said, "Wow . . ."

He shared an anecdote about working on *Welcome to Anhedonia,* an acid-trip web series parody of children's programming. Rodney Anonymous came on set wearing a tweed jacket and ill-fitting collar, commanded the green screen, and delivered a largely improvised, sweaty, and unhinged performance as the "president of College University." The puppets on the show were created by Monkey Boys Productions, later behind the WHYY program *Albie's Elevator*, an indelibly Philly kids' show starring an adorable blue-haired monster muppet. Its first two seasons featured appearances from several local musicians, including Rodney as Albie's imaginary "Rock Hippo," and Joe in full walking-toon regalia as "Pepperoni Sam."

In early November 2013, the Dead Milkmen, Dan Mapp, and Dave Reckner reunited with Howard Kramer, then working for the Rock & Roll Hall of Fame, over dinner in Cleveland. WCSB, one of the country's remaining fiery student-run radio stations out of Cleveland State University, had booked the Milkmen to headline their Halloween Masquerade Ball at Gordon Square theater. Kramer brought the crew to his favorite Vietnamese restaurant, where they chatted like it was old times, talked about their kids, and buried old hatchets. He was grateful to get to know Dandrew and share some stories of Dave Blood.

Around midnight, as the Milkmen were finishing their final checks and anticipation was at a fever pitch, the lights went out. The crowd roared. The younger folks couldn't believe they were getting to see the band. Their older siblings and parents were screaming in excitement to see them for the first time since twenty years (to the day) prior at Peabody's DownUnder. The roaring faded. Something was up.

"The emergency lights went on," said Kramer, who had to get home to his young kids. "I'm like, this isn't merely a power outage. They don't have power. I realized after about fifteen minutes this could descend into *Lord of the Flies* . . .

I think I may have said a quick goodbye to Dan [behind the board]. Like, good luck with this pal. You're gonna need it."

After a few minutes of navigating the mayhem, crowd chatter at deafening levels, it became clear that the power wasn't returning. Stanislav Žabić and Dean plopped down on a bench off to the side of the stage, looked at each other, and not knowing what else to do, laughed. There was no way that, somehow, this wasn't Dave Blood coming back to fuck with them one last time.

These fans came for a show, and a show they would get. As Stanislav was talking to the WCSB coordinators and brewing up plan B, the Milkmen took to the stage under a sea of cell-phone lights. Dean set up a snare drum. Joe and Dan, both in their Halloween costumes, faithfully played their instruments despite nobody being able to hear anything other than the strings clacking. The band busted out an unplugged version of "Beige Sunshine." Rodney screamed, poignantly, "Peer into the edge of time, see the endless light." Dandrew sang his bass lines at the top of his lungs. The whole room unleashed a sing-along of "Punk Rock Girl."

Those who stuck it out were already rewarded, but WCSB and the band were not done. Despite the clocks falling back later that night, an extenuating set of circumstances (the whole block was out for hours), and a long return to Philly the next day, they went to the radio station and played their complete set list. Everybody in Cleveland, and countless more on the internet, got the full Dead Milkmen experience that night. Rodney, taking advantage of the station's safe-harbor hours, swore like a sailor. In an ultimate flex before finally ending the party around 3 a.m., they closed with "Dance with Me." Thirty years had passed, but it felt like they were in Dean's parents' basement again.

In 1990, they'd catalogued Philly's corporate radio takeover on "The Big Sleazy," calling out WXPN's destruction by "folk Nazis." The next year, they saw Andy Chalfen get the boot, along with the rest of the community who rolled the dice on May 6, 1984, and gave them their big on-air break. For the rest of that decade, the dominoes continued falling as NPR expanded its colonization of left-of-the-dial frequencies, squeezing out local talent to play pretty music for pretty people, catering to *fauxhemian* strawmen Rodney screams at in "How Do You Even Manage to Exist?"

On October 3, 2025, Cleveland State University handed over WCSB to Ideastream Public Media, an entity somehow even blander than NPR, who rebranded the station as "JazzNEO." With no advance notice to students or volunteers at the station, CSU President Laura Bloomberg signed an eight-year partnership, surrendering all programming on the 89.3 frequency in exchange for a seat on the Ideastream board and a glut of newspeak underwriting about "strategic collaborations." Bloomberg's "opportunity to grow our engagement" resulted in Cleveland police forcibly escorting the students and volunteers from their station. It was WXPN in 1991 again, only with smooth jazz and an abruptly pulled website, with it going the archived Milkmen anarchy along with five decades of station history. Station leadership picketed the university and started XCSB.org to spread the word and call for reinforcements.

On November 7, as I was on my way to Philadelphia, I got an email from Stanislav. The Dead Milkmen were coming to Cleveland to join the fight. *Can't stop, won't stop.* The first show on January 7, 2026, sold out so quickly, they added a Sunday show, which also sold out almost immediately.

"WCSB announced [at the show] that they have started a nonprofit and revealed intentions of starting a web stream sometime in March and getting their own space in May," wrote Žabić. "When they announced that they filed a lawsuit against CSU, the audience just went nuts—everyone started hugging, high-fiving and celebrating loudly . . . whoever was there will remember this for a long time, especially if WCSB wins the lawsuit."

True to 2026 form, a panoply of videos appeared from their Grog Shop shows capturing the multigenerational ebullience of the room. At one point, the Milkmen—all on vocals—joined local egg-punk openers PAL for a wild performance of Suburban Lawns' "Janitor." Against insurmountable odds and an increasingly contentious world outside those walls, it was unbelievable how much fun they were having—joy on full display as an act of resistance.

Today, the music industry that hobbled the Dead Milkmen has cratered, and the "critical establishment" who told them they weren't serious enough are out of work and writing think pieces on Substack. Society keeps getting some things right while getting other things incredibly wrong, but either way the Dead Milkmen are not done pouring themselves into reminding people of how much is right. Perhaps Joe and Garth were onto something fifty years ago when the imaginary Dead Milkmen emerged from a world-building game that had no conclusion. Dave Blood may be gone, but every time the band plays "Dean's Dream," everyone comes together, no matter what in their life is pissing them off, to scream his words to the rafters: "HE'S ALRIGHT."

We're alright.

EPILOGUE: DAN'S DREAM

"I remember the first time Dandrew was playing that I saw him replacing David," said Sheila Sullivan. "When I was hugging the band [goodbye], I just gave him a big hug, and I said, 'I'm so glad you're here. You know, David would be so proud of you.'"

It was always helpful for Dandrew to hear that from David's old friends. One woman even gifted him one of Dave's old bass picks after a show. Regardless, becoming a member of his favorite band came with years of anxiety and impostor syndrome.

"I always felt like if I were to go see the Dead Milkmen, I wouldn't want to see some other guy playing bass," said Dandrew, "[then I had] the realization that I'm the longest-running bass player. I was looking at some of our fans who were like sixteen, seventeen years old, like, holy shit, I've been the bass player for their whole lives."

Over half a decade into Dandrew's tenure as Dead Milkmen bassist, and twelve years after Dave Blood took his own life, Dave came to Dandrew in a dream.

●

Dandrew calls up Dave Blood, asks if he wants to hang out. He says sure. Dan goes over there. He doesn't have much, just some cigarettes sitting on a table. Dave introduces him to his dog, Mario. They talk about how they both like being cold at night, wearing lots of blankets. Dan mentions electromagnetic fields. Dave gets enthusiastic . . . then it is silent. Dave pushes Play on a nearby cassette tape, and it's some old Dead Milkmen song Dan has never heard: "The Deluge." Dan, thinking it's time to go, starts driving away. He realizes he forgot to say goodbye. He turns around. He sees Dave outside his place, by a concrete pool, and thanks him for hanging out. Sure, says Dave, no problem, and gets on a skateboard. He starts skating in the empty pool. Dan thinks to himself, Why don't I get a photo with him? Hey, I really hate to do this, but can I get a picture with you? Yeah, that's fine, Dave says . . . I'm sure you get asked that a lot too. They take the picture. Suddenly, a flood rushes in. These girls show up and fight over Dan's phone as the deluge covers everything.

"Dave did believe in being able to talk to people after they're gone," added Sheila. "He definitely felt that kind of thing could happen."

ACKNOWLEDGMENTS

The Philadelphia portion of this research was supported by the University of Vermont College of Arts and Sciences Small Grant Award. Thank you to those who welcomed me to their homes and places of business in Philly and beyond: Dean Sabatino, Joe Genaro, Dan Mapp, Joe Carlough, Katie Haegele, and Wesley Hein. Special thanks to Kurt Schulthise and Jennie Dunham for going the extra mile to share David's story.

Gratitude to the murderers' row of personalities who took time and helped make this book what it is: Dan(drew) Stevens, Sam An, Dave Bangert, Nancy Barile, Brian Beattie, Andrew Bentley, Sean Bonnette, Jennifer Brannon, Colin Camerer, Brian Campbell, Andrew Chalfen, Chris Coccia, Doug Conn, Justin Daniel, Cyndy Drue, Andrew Ervin, Brooke Feenie, Stewart Frescas, Atom Goren, J. T. Habersaat, JP Hasson, Hyena Hell, Rick Johnson, Rich Kaufmann, Howard Kramer, MC Lars, Brian McTear, Chuck Meehan, Paul Misner, Seven Morris, Amy Morrissey, Ted Niceley, Al Quint, Bogdan Rakić, Patrick Rapa, David Reckner, Stephane Rowley, Raws Schlesinger, Jay Schwartz, Kyle Shutt, Erica Smith, Ben Snakepit, Sheila Sullivan,

Steve Swart, Colin Vent, Samuel Locke Ward, Sean White, Graham Williams, Jon Wurster, Stanislav and Snežana Žabić, and Carl Zenobi.

I cannot imagine being the writer I am today without decades of wisdom and encouragement from Ted Hornick, Mike Fournier, and Val Paschall. Thank you to Jana and Pam for enduring that rainy Halloween up in Philly so many years ago (RIP to the Troc). Thanks to Jeff Gomez for starting J-Card, Dave Heaton for his sage advice, and Tim Anderl for his outreach.

Thank you, most of all, to my family: my wife, Lisa, for her love and boundless support; my dad for scouring eBay to find that original press of *Big Lizard in My Backyard* all those Christmases ago; and my mom and my sister for going with it.

And finally, I'll never forget where I was—driving down Route 81 in Connecticut one sunny summer Saturday in 2000—that time some Radio 104.1 DJ went off script and played "Punk Rock Girl." He even took a moment to rant about how not enough people appreciated the Dead Milkmen. I can only imagine the earful he got from his bosses. Respect is due.

CHAPTER NOTES

Prologue
"Bar Owner Gets a Year and a Day for Dealing Coke." *Philadelphia Daily News*, 25 June 1987.

Kerr, Jim. "Sabatino's Original Art Works Escape Easy Description." *News Herald* (Perkasie, PA), 16 February 1983.

1. "Prisoner's Cinema"
Adams, Sean. "Rodney Anonymous of the Dead Milkmen: 'Until society can get its act together, we'll have to keep writing songs.'" *PennLive*, 21 October 2014. https://www.pennlive.com/entertainment/2014/10/dead_milkmen_chameleon_club.html.

Albom, Mitch. "Tiger's New Hero Emerges; They're Playing His Song." *Detroit Free Press*, 27 July 1987.

Bittick, Tony. "Philadelphia Band Makes Music Fun." *Central Michigan Life* (Mt. Pleasant, MI), 27 October 1986.

Ellison, Harlan. "Our Little Miss." In Ellison, Harlan, Terry Dowling, Richard Delap, and Gil Lamont. *The Essential Ellison: A 50-Year Retrospective*. Revised and expanded edition. Beverly Hills, CA: Morpheus International, 2001.

Kuipers, Dean. "Spilled Milkmen." *Spin*, June 1990.

Telephone, Justin. "Dead Milkmen." *Razorcake* (Interview), No. 54, 2009.

Wion, Dick. "I Dream of Milkmen." *Daily Illini* (Urbana, IL), 4 March 1994, Diversions.

2. *Music for the Mindless*
Bonner, John. "Mirth Day: The Dead Milkmen Declare a Holiday for Everyone." *Short Cutz*, June 1990.

"Interview with Joe Jack Talcum (Dead Milkmen, Low Budgets)." *Cheap Shot Philly,* 3 February 2011. https://cheapshotphilly.wordpress.com/2011/02/03/interview-with-joe-jack-talcum-dead-milkmen-low-budgets/.

James, Robin, ed. *Cassette Mythos*. New York: Autonomedia, 1992.
Karas, Matty. "Examples of What Too Much TV Can Do." *Asbury Park Press*, 31 May 1989.

Quint, Al. "The Dead Milkmen." Suburban Voice (17), Fall 1985.
Racher, Dave. "Teen Says Pal Kill Door-to-Door Milkman." *Philadelphia Daily News*, 16 October 1981.

Thatcher, Ronald. "Interview with the Parents of Rodney Anonymous of the Dead Milkmen." *Maximumrocknroll* (30), November 1985.

3. "Watching Scotty Die"
Chalfen, Andrew. "On Dave." *City Paper* (Philadelphia), 18–25 March 2004.

Drogin, Bob. "Brothers Indicted in Bucks Dumping." *Philadelphia Inquirer*, 3 May 1983.

4. "Nutrition"
Andersen, Mark, and Mark Jenkins. *Dance of Days: Two Decades of Punk in the Nation's Capital.* Akashic Books, 2009.

Barile, Nancy. *I'm Not Holding Your Coat: My Bruises-and-All Memoir of Punk Rock Rebellion.* New York: Bazillion Points, 2021.

Daly, Andrew. "'Any Distortion Came from the Amp Itself. It Was Considered a Rather Clean Sound Compared to Other Punk Bands': Joe Genaro on Overhead Conversations, Ad-Libs, and Making It Catchy and Funny on the Dead Milkmen's Classic Punk Debut." *Guitar World* (2025). https://www.guitarworld.com/artists/guitarists/the-dead-milkmen-joe-genaro-big-lizard-in-my-backyard.

Hard Times zine, January 1985.

Hiltbrand, David. "The Dead Milkmen: Pranksters of Punk." *Philadelphia Inquirer*, 9 October 1987.

Hurchalla, George. *Going Underground: American Punk 1979–1989.* PM Press, 2016.

5. "Bitchin' Camaro"
Ink Disease zine No. 10, 1986.

Pope, John. "Hooks Raps Reagan for Apartheid Stand." *New Orleans Times-Picayune.* 21 August 1985.

Rea, Steven. "The 'Weirdest Supercult' Prepares to Gather the Flock." *Philadelphia Enquirer*, 4 May 1985.

6. "Big Time Operator"
Collins, Huntley. "David Wildmann, Avant-Garde Music Promoter (Obituary)." *Philadelphia Inquirer*, 5 June 1988.

In Yer Ear zine, 1989.

MacQueen, Steve. "Glass Eye Returns to Scorch Finale's a Third Time." *Tallahassee Democrat*, 21 July 1987.

Popson, Tom. "Cruising California with Rodney and the Dead Milkmen." *Chicago Tribune*, 28 August 1987.

RIP Magazine, May 1987.

7. "Punk Rock Girl"
Eddy, Chuck. "Dead Milkmen vs. Thelonious Monster: Battle of the Lame" (*Spin* 1987; reprinted in *Terminated for Reasons of Taste*). Duke University Press, 2016.

Gladstone, Jim. "Dead Milkmen Appear at TLA" *Philadelphia Inquirer*, 10 December 1988.

8. "All Around the World"
Gross, Joe. *Fugazi: In on the Kill Taker.* 33 1/3 series, vol. 129. Bloomsbury, 2018.

"Interview with Rodney Anonymous (Dead Milkmen)." *Cheap Shot Philly*, 3 February 2011. https://cheapshotphilly.wordpress.com/2011/02/03/interview-with-rodney-anonymous-dead-milkmen/. Prindle, Mark. "Dave Blood." Interview at https://www.markprindle.com/blood-i.htm, 2003.

Telephone, Justin. "Dead Milkmen." *Razorcake* (Interview), No. 54, 2009.

9. "I Started to Hate You"
Fricke, David. "The Dookie Chronicles." *Rolling Stone* (1204), 13 March 2014.

10. "I Can't Stay Awake"
Rapa, Patrick. "Blood Brothers: The Dead Milkmen Return to Pay Tribute to the Late Dave Schulthise." *City Paper*, 11–18 November 2004.

Shaw, Deirdre. "Ex-Rocker Takes on Role of Refugee from Serbia." *Philadelphia Enquirer*, 25 April 1999.

Vanderwal, Karrin. "The Dead Milkmen: How to Become a Serial Killer and Other Absolute Gibberish." *Flipside*, 1994.

11. "Meaningless Upbeat Happy Song"
MacQueen, Ken. "The Dead Milkmen: Stoney's Extra Stout Pig." Music Review, *Vancouver Sun*, 9 November 1995.

Takiff, Jonathan. "Stoney's Extra Stout Pig." Music Review, *Philadelphia Daily News*, 25 October 1995.

12. "Welcome to the End of the World"
Tugade, Amanda F. "Two Afrikaner Families from South Africa Classified as Refugees Arrive in Iowa." *Des Moines Register*. 14 May 2025. https://www.desmoinesregister.com/story/news/2025/05/14/afrikaner-refugees-iowa-south-africa/83621981007/.